AN UNTIDY CAREER

CONVERSATIONS WITH GEORGE HALL

Lolly Susi

An Untidy Career
Conversations with George Hall

OBERON BOOKS
LONDON

First published in 2010 by Oberon Books Ltd
521 Caledonian Road, London N7 9RH
Tel: 020 7607 3637 / Fax: 020 7607 3629
e-mail: info@oberonbooks.com
www.oberonbooks.com

The Publisher is grateful to the Central School of Speech and Drama for its
co-operation in publishing this book. In particular, we thank the principal,
Professor Gavin Henderson CBE.

Cover photograph courtesy of Central School of Speech & Drama

Images in text courtesy of the Central School of Speech & Drama
Wimbledon School of Theatre Design, Wimbledon College of Art

Every effort has been made to trace the copyright holders of all images
reprinted in this book. Acknowledgement is made in all cases where the
image source is available, but we would be grateful for information about any
images where sources could not be traced.

ISBN: 978-1-84002-989-5

Printed in Great Britain by CPI Antony Rowe, Chippenham

Contents

'You will always have an untidy career, but you could well become a complete man of the theatre.'

Michel Saint-Denis

George Hall graduated from Michel Saint-Denis' Old Vic Theatre School in 1951 and his subsequent career has included work as a music hall performer, cabaret artist, actor, director, songwriter, teacher and singing coach. He has been a musical director for BBC-TV, taught at some of the most prestigious colleges in the world, performed on Sunday Night at the Palladium, lectured at international theatre conferences, and was a founding member of the Piccolo Theatre and the 59 Theatre Company at the Lyric, Hammersmith. As musical director, he was part of the team of innovative theatre practitioners that ran the Old Vic Theatre the year before it became home to the National Theatre. This same group went on to create the 69 Theatre Company, now known as the Royal Exchange Theatre, in Manchester.

For nearly a quarter century, George was Head of the acting course at the Central School of Speech and Drama, and his ex-students have had successful careers in all aspects of theatre, television and film—many going on to earn BAFTAs, Oliviers, Oscars, Tonys and Golden Globes. Alongside some of the world's foremost cabaret artists and musical directors, George still serves on the faculty of the Cabaret Conference at Yale University in America, and he continues to teach and direct at the Royal Academy of Music and the Guildhall School of Music and Drama.

I first met George Hall when I auditioned for a place on the acting course at the Central School. Having heard of the training from a friend, within days I had sent off my application, quit my job as an actress with the Hawaii Theatre Festival and booked my flight to London. Shortly before I was to leave, I received a letter saying that Central had accepted their quota of ten women for the coming year. With the blind optimism of youth and vague plans to 'find a tutor', I hitched up my backpack and got on the plane anyway.

Within days of my arrival, I was introduced to Central tutor John Jones, who agreed to take me as a private student. He must have seen some tiny glimmer of possibility, for he soon arranged a special audition for the school and I was asked to attend a recall two weeks later. After a morning of performing speeches, an afternoon of improvisation and movement, then more work on my speeches before a panel of staff, by late afternoon I was a mass of nerves, exhaustion and despair. How could I ever have dreamt I could earn a place at Central?

When I was called into a private meeting with George, I knew that it was a defining moment in my life. George beamed at me, as only George can beam: "We were going to take ten girls, but we're now going to take eleven." My flood of tears was followed by body-wracking sobs.

George's face crumbled in confusion. "I don't think you understand," he soothed. "We're accepting you as the eleventh girl?"

"*I kno-ooow…!*" I howled.

After I finished my training, I would often see George and John's supportive faces in the audience—whether in dingy little fringe theatres or large West End venues. When George invited me to return to Central as a freelance director and teacher, he opened up a fulfilling sideline to my life as an actor.

George continues to have an effect on my life, just as he remains a strong positive influence on the lives and careers of many of his ex-students, some of whom have contributed to this book. Hollywood director, Peter Chelsom, wrote, 'I channel George all the time in my work as a film director. So many times I have the thought, "What George could do with this actor in one afternoon!"' Actress Zoe Wanamaker, CBE, says, 'The theatre has magic, but George deciphers it in a way that is clear, that has life and joy.' Sara Kestelman, actress and writer, adds, 'The contribution that George has made to the theatre industry, and to several generations of actors and performers, is beyond value; his dedication, passion and commitment to the industry has helped to produce some of the finest proponents of acting that the United Kingdom is proud to honour, enjoy and celebrate.'

It seems a little like cheating to have enjoyed myself so much in the creation of this manuscript. George and his partner of over forty years, John Jones, are consummate hosts. While John prepared lunch in the kitchen of their Brighton flat, George and I chatted in the front room, in the corner of which sits the white baby grand piano bought with proceeds from George's glittery Central retirement show at the Duke of York's Theatre in 1986. (John still irreverently refers to this event as 'Hall Aid'.) The walls of every room in their seaside flat are lined with books, albums, tapes and CDs. Whether to illuminate a point or just to share his delight in a favourite performer who has created a memorable moment, George cannot refrain from playing a cherished recording. If he can't find what he is looking for, or if he can't remember a name, it's: 'Johnny! Where…?' or 'Johnny! Who…?' Their relationship is full of easy wit and fun: 'Did you know there is a grammar case that grammarians don't know? John uses it and it's called the "disguised imperative." "Shall you bring me a chocolate?" …The answer could be no, but one knows better.'

It wasn't easy to convince George to do this book: 'Darling, I'm not sure I have anything to say that anyone would be the least interested in hearing….' I'm glad I persevered. Even so, it was often a struggle to get George to focus on himself. His and John's enthusiasm for their latest projects—and their pride in hundreds of current and ex-students from all over the world—peppered conversations with "Did you see…? You must!' 'What did you think? Wasn't she marvellous?' 'Brilliant, darling.' George's main criticism of the following manuscript has always been: 'But I must tell you about them; this really shouldn't be all about me!"

For the first time, I'm afraid, I tried not to listen to his advice.

The following 'conversation' incorporates material from George's lectures and articles but is compiled mostly from a number of interviews over a period of many months. I have edited liberally for clarity and continuity, but I hope I have maintained even a fraction of this extraordinary man's personality, wit and humour, his scope and intelligence—and the warmth of his very big heart.

Lolly: I've known you for a long time, George, but I know very little about your early life. I suppose we'd better start at the beginning. You were born in a district of Edinburgh called Polwarth to William and Ann in 1925. Tell me about your parents? Your childhood?

George: My father fought in WWI, then became the branch manager of a grocery co-op, but he was extremely well read in both literature and history. My mother left school when she was fourteen to become a 'clerkess' in my father's store, which is where they met. She was quite brilliant mathematically: if I were to say, 'I'm doing something on the 16th of April,' she'd say, 'That's a Thursday this year.' I never understood how she did that.

I was an only child, though I was part of a close and extended family, and from about the age of ten, I went to Heriot's, which is in the centre of Edinburgh. George Heriot had been jeweller to James VI of Scotland, later James I of England, and had left a small fortune to found this school for 'fatherless bairns'. The school then turned into what I suppose in England would be called a grammar school, but when I was a student there were still a lot of kids whose fathers had died. Fees were really very small—but very big for my parents. Of course, I rebelled against the place when I was there, but looking back it was an amazing school with a lot of splendid teachers. I finished in 1942 and was waiting to be called up for the forces, so they made a one-person arts course for me. Can you imagine? I assisted the music teacher that year and he gave me my first experience of teaching.

I'd taken private music lessons at Heriot's from when I was eleven until I was eighteen and the music teacher always took me perfectly seriously, but he got much more interested one day when he said, 'This really should be in a different key.' I said, 'Well, that's no problem.' And it wasn't. And it never has been. As a result, he and my parents thought I ought to have a career as a music teacher, but I kept wondering how I could I get out of it. I always wanted to go into the theatre.

Lolly: Always? How did that come about for the son of a co-op manager?

George: At the age of six or seven—these are such nonsense things, aren't they?—somebody asked me what I wanted to be and I said, 'A producer of plays.' I don't know how I had ever heard that phrase, but I was quite sure that's what I wanted to do. My parents were always very supportive and I was taken to pantomime from the time I was five; and one of my parents knew the manager of the Theatre Royal in Edinburgh, so we regularly got Monday night tickets. Then from the time I was eleven, I went to the theatre on my own. I went to a Rachmaninov piano recital, and when I was standing at the stage door he came out and patted my head!

I saw people who are probably not remembered by anybody alive. There were lots of people who had stopped performing by the time of the war—Florrie Ford, a lot of local Scottish comics. The performers were all local working class and there was no real social division between them and the audience. As a result, English comics didn't go down well in Scotland and Scottish comics couldn't flourish down here or even in the north of England. Saying that, there were also wonderful Scottish comics like Harry Lauder, who had a great reputation all over the world.

The first straight play I remember seeing was *Love on the Dole*, with Wendy Hiller, at the Empire Theatre in the mid-'30s;

and the thing that amazed me was that there was a sink with taps with real water—I was terribly taken with that. I also clearly remember Gielgud and Marie Tempest in something called *Dear Octopus*. Then, early during the war, I walked on in a touring production of Barrie's *What Every Woman Knows*, starring Dame Irene Vanbrugh. I remember her vividly. She was very old school and I'm sure her performance didn't vary much from night to night, but she was wonderful and rather glittery.

Lolly: I am often less impressed now with performers that I loved when I was younger. Styles move on, but our tastes move on as well.

George: Yes, and you can have a shock seeing a favourite movie when you haven't seen it for a while.

Lolly: Did you see a lot of films?

George: Oh, yes. We went at least once a week and I often went alone to Saturday morning movies. I saw one Fred Astaire film three times around, until my distraught parents appeared with the usherette: 'If he's not here…!' And of course, we used to listen to radio programmes all the time—dance bands, the plays, children's hour. By the end of the '30s the BBC had had a huge effect, so you got the Big Bands touring the halls— Henry Hall's Band, Jack Paine's Band. All of that contributed to my idea that I wanted to be in the theatre.

Then, when I was thirteen my two best friends did a puppet show of Cinderella. They were awfully good with their hands and made puppets: I wasn't good with my hands and didn't make puppets, so I wrote the songs. That means I wrote my first song over seventy years ago! How is that possible?

But my first real opportunity came about as a result of these absolutely marvellous classes that the Royal Scottish Museum started on a Saturday morning. When the war closed the museum, the class was transferred to the National Gallery of Scotland. Of course, the most valuable of paintings were taken away and I think buried in Wales, but they had a handful of things left, and every week this small group of children would turn up and artists would take us round and talk about the art. I got the most terrific visual education from it. I wrote a show for that group in 1940 for a war charity. That was a wonderful era if you had any show biz ambitions, as you suddenly were given a huge excuse to perform—war effort forever! While I was still a student, I directed Chekhov's *The Proposal* and a great horror piece by W. W. Jacobs called *The Monkey's Paw*.

Lolly: And you continued to see a lot of theatre during the war?

George: Everybody toured. I saw Noël Coward, the Lunts. I knew I was part of history when one of my American students asked me, 'What is a Lunt?'

Then I went to London for a visit, just before I was called up for the Air Force in '43. All the theatres had closed when the war started and when the Sadler's Wells Ballet (now the Royal) first reopened they only did matinees, with maybe one evening a week. People got used to it, of course. People get used to everything. When there were doodlebugs there'd be an air raid warning: you'd hear the sirens, and they'd say 'Anybody who wants to leave, do so now,' but mostly nobody did. When the all clear sounded everybody would cheer, but if no 'all clear' sounded and it got to the end of the play, very often the cast would entertain the audience.

I saw masses of wonderful plays during the Blitz: *Arsenic and Old Lace*, *Uncle Vanya*, which was the first Chekhov I'd ever seen, *Sweet and Low* with Hermione Gingold. I saw Michael Redgrave in *A Month in the Country*, and Sybil Thorndike in *Lottie Dundas*, *Peer Gynt* with Ralph Richardson, and Olivier in *Richard III*—and both of them in *Arms and the Man* and *Uncle Vanya*. Olivier's *Richard III* with the Old Vic Company was fantastic on stage, a million times better than his film. Olivier's physical presence was astounding. You know he thought *Richard III* was going to be a disaster? Apparently before the curtain went up, he went onstage and looked at the auditorium and said 'Fuck you all.' Of course, it wasn't a disaster and he jumped up ten rungs of the ladder overnight.

Then from August to October of 1945, I was stationed at Chigwell in Essex, which meant I could get into London in the evening even though I didn't have a pass to do so. I went to the reopened Sadler's Wells—a season headed by Fonteyn and Helpmann—and I saw Gielgud's company do *A Midsummer Night's Dream* and *Hamlet* and *The Duchess of Malfi*, starring Gielgud and Ashcroft. At the end of the war in Europe, on VE night, I was in London seeing Fonteyn and Helpmann in *Coppelia*.

Lolly: What was your job in the Air Force?

George: I was first in an operational unit in Lincolnshire doing Morse code to people who were flying over Germany on raids. Then they found they could send Morse at two hundred words a minute by speeding it up and then slowing it down at the other end, so I was trained in high-speed telegraphy.

When the war in Europe finished in spring of '45 everything focused on the war in the Far East. I was to be sent to India, but just before I was supposed to go they dropped the atom bomb and by the time I got there they didn't need me anymore, so I had three months in Bombay where I went to the swimming pool every day. Then we drove from Bombay to Madras and on to Singapore, where I worked for six months. We were then sent to Cairo, but they didn't need us there either, so they sent us to Rome, on to Naples via Malta, and then to a village outside Graz in Austria. I lived there for about fifteen months.

Lolly: Yet you still managed to see some theatre during that period?

George: Shortly after I was posted to Austria in the autumn of '46 I had a leave, and en route to Edinburgh I stopped briefly in London. I remember queuing at the New Theatre, which was a curious system whereby one could buy a ticket early in the morning for a six-penny stool and the numbered stools were then set out an hour before the performance so one could reclaim one's place. That evening I saw Olivier in *King Lear*, the next afternoon I saw *Lear* again and that evening Hermione Gingold in *Sweetest and Lowest*. Then I took the night train to Edinburgh, where I saw the Ballet Champs Elysees, and then on to Glasgow to see *Antony and Cleopatra* with Edith Evans and Godfrey Turl—not entirely successful, but the witty bits were fantastic and Edith created female mischief as a kind of allure.

Really, by the time I went to the Old Vic Theatre School, I'd seen a lot of theatre, and I think I didn't work as hard as I should as a student because I still went to the theatre all the time.

Lolly: How did you end up at the Old Vic Theatre School?

George: Really, the feeling in the immediate post-war period was quite euphoric. The experience of the war had convinced a huge working class that they hadn't had their share of the goodies and they decided they were never going to go back to that. The Atlee government had come in. There was going to be a national health service. Bevin, as well as being the Health Minister, brought forward something called 'the six-penny rate', which meant that up to six pence per pound of the local rates councils charged could be spent on arts and amenities. Theatre had started to become de-centralised in a way it had never been before. The Arts Council was born, and repertory companies started up all over the country.

Olivier and Richardson had been the Directors of the Old Vic Theatre and it was arranged that following the war Michel Saint-Denis would take it over and run something called the Old Vic Centre. The Old Vic Theatre itself was going to be an experimental theatre—that part never got off the ground. There would be a school run by Glen Byam Shaw, who was a big West End director; and they would start a touring company for children, the Young Vic, that would be run by George Devine—who was an up and coming director and had been managing director of Motley. They were all going to teach at the school and Percy Harris from Motley was going to be Head of Design.

I knew I was entitled to a generous government grant for education upon demobilization, so I applied to the Old Vic School and got an interview when I was on a leave from Austria in 1947 and was accepted on the Technical Production course for the autumn of 1947. But demobilization was deliberately slow. If everybody in the forces had come onto the labour market at the same time, there would have been absolute chaos. Therefore you were demobbed on the basis of how much your trade was needed. Unfortunately what I did was still needed, so I had to wait until November '47 to be demobbed and the Vic School deferred my acceptance until '48.

Lolly: How did you hear about the Vic School when you were in Austria?

George: It was terribly well publicized—very much in the air—and the people concerned were so notable. Michel Saint-Denis had done a very famous *Three Sisters* in the '30s; and he'd just done *Oedipus* with Olivier in an Old Vic season of Olivier and Richardson at the New Theatre. But I can't really talk about Michel without first telling you about his uncle, Jacques Copeau.

Copeau was very much a force in the French theatre during the early part of the 20th century. He had been disillusioned by what was on offer in Paris—mostly either empty boulevard comedies done with great panache and skill but saying nothing, or plays done in the very dead tradition of the Comédie Francaise where if you took over a part that somebody else had played for twenty years, your excellence was measured by how indistinguishable it was from the previous performer. So in 1913, Copeau opened his own theatre on the Left Bank, the Théâtre du Vieux-Colombier and he worked as an actor, playwright and translator.

Then, for the duration of World War One, Copeau closed the theatre and went to New York. When he returned in 1920, his nephew, Michel, joined the company as a stage manager and assistant. In '24, with a company of thirty actors—the 'Copiaus'—Copeau went to Pernand-Vergelesses in Burgundy to establish an acting school. He really set out to train actors for a new kind of theatre: he focused on physical work, music and mime, and he devised exercises for actors to study and re-create the movement of animals.

Five years later, Copeau disbanded the Copiaus and returned to Paris—oddly enough to run the Comédie Francaise—and with part of the remaining group Michel founded a successor company, the Compagnie des Quinze. They worked on voice and continued work on movement, mime, masks and animal study. They had always developed their own scripts, but Copeau introduced Michel to the playwright, André Obey, who joined the company and helped to shape productions into a more dramatic form. It was this collaboration that created *Noé*, or *Noah*.

When *Noah* and the other play in their repertoire, *Le Viol de Lucrèce*, came to the Arts Theatre Club in 1931, they were a sensation. I once asked Peggy Ashcroft about the reaction to the first night of *Noah* and she told me they were overcome by the physicality and by the singing, by the wonderful diction and use of language—and by the totally original staging. Michel cast a spell with that play. Olivier and Gielgud went mad over the Compagnie des Quinze.

The actor, Marius Goring, had worked with Michel in Burgundy so introduced him into a group of people who used to meet at the Motley studio, and Michel became very friendly with them all.

Lolly: What was the Motley studio?

George: Well, Motley was a three-person design team: two sisters—Margaret Harris (who was always called Percy) and Sophie Harris (who married George Devine); and their art school friend, Elizabeth Montgomery. They had first made themselves known to John Gielgud in the '30s by standing at the stage door and shyly giving him sketches of himself. From that, Gielgud, who had an extremely keen visual sense, started to use them as designers. Percy and Elizabeth went to Hollywood during the war and Elizabeth stayed there, but anything that any of the three of them did was always credited as 'by Motley'.

Their studio in the '30s was in a small lane in the West End opposite the Coward Theatre. It had been the workshop of the 18th century cabinetmaker, Thomas Chippendale, and they learned that Chippendale had liked actors dropping in for a drink or a cup of chocolate, so they began to serve afternoon teas on a big scale. Actors, directors, designers, artists of all types would drop in; and it became a great social centre, a gathering place for the theatrical establishment that was unhappy with the West End—and particularly not happy with the well-meant but hideous-looking productions that had been going on at the Old Vic in the '30s, where if a director spent fifteen shillings on a production, the theatre owner, Lillian

Bayliss, had a heart attack. They thought theatre had to become more tempting.

At these afternoon teas you could find people like Peggy Ashcroft, Edith Evans, John Gielgud, Laurence Olivier, Michael Redgrave. Percy Harris once told me that in 1930-whatever, they spent £5 a week on tea and cakes. In those days! Amazing hospitality. So when the Compagnie des Quinze was such a success, Michel was called into that ambience.

Gielgud was very anxious to extend himself—until the end of his life he was one of the great experimenters of the British theatre—so he persuaded Michel to do an English production of *Noah* so that he could play the main part. Percy Harris created the costumes, but she did it all for tuppence so they were cut so badly that the actors could hardly move. George Devine told me a dreadful story once: he wore the bear costume, which was incredibly heavy and made him sweat gallons, and he swore that he took it off and left it on its side by the dressing room heater and when he came in the next day it was standing up. Isn't that awful?

Gielgud was not really good casting to play Noah, and actors like Alec Guinness, Harry Andrews and George Devine had had no real physical preparation for the task of playing animals. It was in fact a bit crazy to try to do *Noah* with an English cast. The original production had grown out of months and months of studio work in France: in London Michel only had about three weeks rehearsal—with actors who had never been asked to be bears or penguins and didn't know where to start. Michel was a bit appalled by their lack of physical skills. But out of this, more and more people said that Michel should come here to work permanently and found a training school.

Lolly: Why do you think he made the decision to leave France?

George: Michel was very attracted by something in the English temperament. He said that the English had this wonderful

balance between reality and style, whereas the French got
trapped in style. In France, he felt you couldn't do anything
without it become an 'ism'—it was somehow immediately
'Impressionism' or 'Cubism'—and he was attracted by
something rather wonderfully muddled about English thought
that didn't desire a high-powered definition. Also, Peggy
Ashcroft told me, a little slyly, that Michel was always going to
be regarded as Copeau's nephew in France. Apparently when
she did *Three Sisters* with Michel, Copeau visited and gave her
some notes—and Michel was beside himself with rage.

Michel started a studio here, first of all doing classes for very
established actors, then in 1935—with the support of people
like Gielgud and Olivier, Tyrone Guthrie, Charles Laughton
and Marius Goring—he opened the London Theatre Studio in
some terrible rented rehearsal space in the West End. The next
year, George Devine and Glen Byam Shaw helped him set up
the London Theatre Studio in its own space in Islington.

It had a real impact. It was extremely innovative—training not
only actors but directors and designers, as well—and it turned
out some distinguished students. Jocelyn Herbert had done
art school training, but she went to the Studio to learn—to
absorb—the theatre training that Michel gave. He continued
to give a lot of classes for professional actors, but there was also
an intake of new students. Peter Ustinov was a particularly
naughty one. He learnt to impersonate Michel's broken
English and caused great mayhem by phoning up and altering
arrangements: 'This is Michel. Classes have been cancelled.'

The Studio existed until 1939 and the outbreak of war,
when Michel got this curious job as 'Jacques Duchesne'—
broadcasting nightly to the free French underground and
coaching Churchill to make speeches in his not very good
French. Michel used to tell of a particular occasion when they
both got terribly drunk and he sat on Churchill's knee while

broadcasting to the French underground. It must have made for a very lively broadcast.

Copeau died in 1941, and when the war finished Michel was offered the directorship of the Comédie Francaise. He turned it down: he wanted to stay in England. That's when he started the Old Vic Theatre School, which was due to start in 1946. But the Old Vic Theatre was terribly decrepit and it wasn't ready until January 1947, so the first group only did five terms and spent their first year in Baron's Court in what became the Royal Ballet School. The Old Vic Theatre had been damaged by bombs in about 1940 and was closed; but even after it opened as a school there were rats, there was no carpeting, you weren't allowed to walk in the Circle because you might fall through the holes in the floor, there was no seating.

When I started in 1948 on the Technical Production course, we were at the Old Vic; then in December 1949 we left for an adapted girls' school in Dulwich for my remaining five terms on the Acting Course. The school's theatre in Dulwich did the best with what would have been a school hall and it's a shame Michel never had the chance to have exactly the theatre he wanted. He would have loved Copeau's idea of an inner stage, two levels, and wing doors like in Restoration theatre. He wanted the architecture to be the set, so you put images in it but not the literal elements, and you didn't try to create a stage picture.

Lolly: What did the Technical Production course entail?

George: Michel wanted to create this new tribe of 'artist technicians' who would be totally in the life of the play, who even if they were only raising the curtain would do it with the feel of the play, the rhythm of the play, and an awareness of its intentions. Michel wanted everyone to learn to envisage entire productions.

Lolly: Up until that point, stagehands were carpenters or electricians and perhaps previously had nothing to do with the theatre. Am I right in thinking that, until the '50s, directors even designed the lights?

George: Yes, but there was only very primitive lighting and very primitive sound. Stage managers and the person on the book had always been around. In fact, in Victorian times directors were called stage managers, later they were called 'producers'. Only recently have they been called directors. In fact, directing then was regarded as fairly utilitarian.

On the tech course we did a lot of lighting and mundane things like scale drawing. We did a bit of sound, a lot of history of the theatre, and quite a bit of script analysis. But the most exciting part of that course for me was Percy Harris. She was wonderful—teaching one about stage space and historical research. If you were considered very good in your first year on the technical course you were asked to stay on for a second year, which was either a directors course or a more detailed designers course. Stage managers and designers shared many classes, and the designers learnt every kind of craft: dyeing, cutting, prop making, scene painting. The course turned out people who went on to amazing careers.

Sandy Wilson, who wrote *The Boy Friend*, was on the tech course along with me, as was Val May, who later ran the Bristol Old Vic. Sandy, Val and I wanted to do a review—so we wrote a great deal of material to be performed by the rest of our year. Sandy had just had a great success in the West End with his material for Hermione Gingold and she was the guest of honour for this Sunday night show. There were no seats in the Vic, so we found a throne for a pre-war *Cleopatra* production— Miss Gingold sat in that with a great sense of it being her due.

I still remember a lot of Sandy's songs:

Take me back to the Waterloo Road,

Where I wasn't a pro
And they didn't mind me asking
All the things I didn't know.

Take me back to the Waterloo Road,
Where the theatre was fun
And you didn't have to worry
If the show was going to run.

I want to have that morning break again,
Eat that canteen cake again
And boast the things I'll do in 1952.

I'll say goodbye to my visions of fame
And the future be blowed,
If you'll just take me back
To the Waterloo Road.

And:

I want to be an actor.
I want to be a celebrated star.
I want to see them queuing
For whatever show I'm doing.
And I want to own a house that has a private bar.

I want to be in 'Hamlet'
And give it something Gielgud has lacked.
I want the Vic to ask me if I'll star at the New

I want to have a knighthood
And my name in Who's Who.

I want to be insulted in a Gingold review.
And, incidentally, I want to act.

Then for the end of year show, George Devine, who was a
director for the school and who had a fantastic feel for physical
comedy, devised an piece for between a double bill of *Right
You Are (If You Think So)* and *The Clandestine Marriage*. The
curtain came down and went up again; I was in the Lillian
Bayliss box with a piano and played a sort of 18ᵗʰ century piece
of music for the bow; then there was feigned panic. A fly bar
came down and somebody held on to it just as it shot back up,
and they all acted that the curtain had fouled. An actor playing
a stage manager said, 'We'll have to do the scene change with
the curtain up,' and then they did what was like a five-minute
Buster Keaton film while I played a silent movie improvisation
on the piano. People carried flats towards each other across
the stage, and there was somebody coming downstage; and as
the flat would cross, he would disappear. Then as the next flat
would cross, he would appear again.

Apropos of this, in 1958 there was a French review called *La
Plume de Ma Tante* by a man called Robert Dhery. It was
brilliant slapstick. George Devine, who by this time was
revered as the guru of new writing at the Royal Court, came
into Joan Plowright's dressing room, slumped down and said,
'That's what I've wanted to do all my life.' Well, I tell you, he
did it wonderfully.

Anyway, the lure of performing proved too great for me. So I
auditioned for the acting course and was accepted.

Ann Morrish and Powys Thomas had been in the first group
of actors. And June Brown—Dot from 'Eastenders'. She was

"George always had a marvellous sense of humour, and even then was always the person that other students went to for his opinion; he seemed so much more knowledgeable than the rest of us. When we had to do a test piece—a speech or a scene for the staff to criticise—George would be very helpful with his notes in rehearsals. You felt warmed by his appreciation, by his approval, but he also knew what things should be and when they weren't right. You knew what he said would be honest and you would believe it to be totally true. He had a very bright mind. In fact, he was a director. He was a good actor, but I think he always wanted really to be in charge of something!"

Dame Joan Plowright, DBE, The Lady Olivier

a raving a beauty. She wasn't just a pretty girl: she was a startling beauty. My year had Prunella Scales, Mike Morgan—a wonderful actor—and Joan Plowright. It was a strong year. Joannie had a hard time, though the course was absolutely perfect for her. But then, it was difficult in many ways. Most of the girls were very young, and many of the men were much older. I was twenty-four, while Patrick Wymark, who became a very well known actor, had done something very important like command a ship during the war.

The Vic deliberately recruited from the widest of social backgrounds. They weren't interested in what your accent was when you arrived, which schools like RADA and Central had always been. The concept now is that you are able to lose your accent onstage, but you keep your offstage accent. In those days, everybody lost their accent—some more successfully than others. Plowright still hasn't got it right! I was broadly Scottish and I did lose my accent at the Vic, but then I think I was around there longer than anybody. When I left, they gave us a written piece of paper as a reference and Glen Byam Shaw, the Head of the acting course, wrote in what I could only see as a weary hand: 'This student has been with us a long, long time.'

Lolly: What was Glen Byam Shaw's background?

George: He had been a very up-and-coming young actor in the 1930s—he played Armand to Tallulah Bankhead's Marguerite in *La Dame aux Camélles*—then he was injured in the war and decided he wouldn't act again. He was rather smoother than Michel. More commercial.

I tell you, the whole place was seething with talent. The Head of the tech course, Cecil Clarke, had been a stage manager before the war and was a fantastic organizer, so by mid-1945 he was doing some very important job coordinating supplies to Berlin. He went on to be the director of Tennant Television. Stephen Arlen, who was the Vic Manager, took over the direction of Sadler's Wells and was responsible for that company moving to the Coliseum. One of the design teachers, Riette Sturge-Moore, designed a lot for the Royal Shakespeare Company. The place was awash with talent and what they did represented an enormous altruistic step away from their careers and earning power. They really all slaved for pittance and yet brought with them great riches of talent.

Lolly: As a student, did you have much contact with Michel Saint-Denis?

George: He gave inspiring talks to us every week. We'd all come from such narrow backgrounds and Michel brought in a sense of the world theatre and an enormous range of thinking.

He loved to talk about the time in 1922 that Stanislavski brought the Moscow Art Theatre to Paris in *The Cherry Orchard*. Michel was hugely under the spell of the French theatre, naturally, and above everything else, there was the Diaghilev Ballet. Michel was enthralled by *Les Noces*, which is a ballet about a Russian wedding, but in a way about all Russian weddings—more about the ritual than about any particular individuals. So with *The Cherry Orchard* Michel thought he was going to see what he called 'the mud of naturalism'. Then Anya entered in the first act, and there was that moment of her being in her own home again, and it was just overwhelming. He said, 'So after we saw Moscow Arts in *Cherry Orchard*, Stanislavski and I wandered the streets of Paris all night and talked.' It was so exciting to hear about that when I was a young student.

Lolly: Here is 'the man' who touched 'the man'. So, Michel was saying, 'Stanislavski has it right. I've seen it work.'

George: Yes, but equally, from his point of view Stanislavski didn't face the problem of what Michel always called 'the written style'. The way I interpret that is this: if you see *West Side Story*, part of your pleasure is the drama, but if somebody is immensely dramatic but out of tune, you will not enjoy it. In a sense, if you see a Shakespeare or a Congreve it's got to be real, but part of your pleasure is also in the actors' expertise, their sensibility and language. You're having two distinct pleasures.

Lolly: An actor might be incredibly natural, very real, and completely in touch…

George: …And yet not realize that half the effect is musical. Michel thought that with the Stanislavski process you could very well finish up with a Shakespeare play that might as well be prose. If you're speaking non-naturalistically, Stanislavski doesn't quite address how you'd reconcile the 'written style'. Michel had wanted actors who could do 'big style' with an authentic inner reality, but without 'the mud of naturalism'. Reality and form—but in balance.

That was Michel's great thing, but it often made him style mad. When I was at Central in the late '60s, Michel had a conference on the world theatre—a very grandiose idea—and we all traipsed to Stockholm for this conference on 'Style'. It was awful. He and the American, John Houseman—who ran Julliard and was a great disciple of Michel's—got themselves in a terrible linguistic tangle. They talked about the 'Pinter style'. Well, Michel really knew that style was the outcome of investigating all the elements, but he could easily sound as if he thought there was 'a way' to do Pinter. And he'd have jumped on anyone who said there was a 'Shakespeare style'. They could get themselves terribly wrong.

Personally, I love de-mystification of the process. When we were doing *Hay Fever* for the television, somebody asked about the 'style' and Edith Evans said, 'Style? We must all do it as if we're Noël.' Wonderful.

But there was sheer inspiration in Michel's lectures and talks at the Vic. And we always knew his intention. We were not being trained for the theatre of Shaftesbury Avenue; we were there to change the theatre—which was both a good and a bad thing. After the school had been going for three years, a lot of senior actors from the profession took Glen Byam Shaw aside and said, 'You know, your students are terribly arrogant.' And we were. We thought: 'You poor souls. You're in yesterday's theatre, and we're tomorrow's theatre. Can't you pull your socks up and just listen to us?' And so the training had to be modified because we were over-aware of how much we carried the flag of the future theatre.

Lolly: The Vic School did have an enormous impact on the theatre.

George: Yes, but the training certainly wasn't perfect. I think the voice work was *fundamentally* good at the Vic, but the speech work wasn't good enough. I really spent years thinking about breathing and voice training after I left, because I didn't get it there. I do think Jani Strasser was a fantastic voice coach. He was from Vienna and was one of the people who, in about 1933, along with the German conductor Fritz Busch and Carl Ebert, a famous German producer, were brought here by John Christie when he started Glyndebourne. As students we learned a lot from Jani but—and I don't think it was just me—nobody understood what he was saying most of the time. He had so many images that were terribly private. He went on about these 'poodles', which I never understood.

Lolly: In terms of breathing? Sound production? What?

George: I have no idea. Something about his poodles. They were conditioned to know when it was time for breakfast, when it was time for a walk. And you were supposed to have conditioned all this apparatus—your 'poodles'. At crit sessions, Jani would say cryptic things, 'The poodles were da-da-da', and Michel would look indulgent, as though a brilliant nephew was saying something, but he didn't know what Jani was talking about either.

Lolly: Is Michel's book, *Promises and Premises*, an accurate account of the training?

George: Really, I think Michel's notion of what he did at the school and what he actually did could be very different.

Lolly: He wrote about a course in comedy technique. Is there such a thing?

George: I didn't think the comedy technique classes were very good: they were terribly heavy-handed. But Joannie Plowright thought they were wonderful so, you know, we all had different experiences. I must have interviewed hundreds of people to teach at Central and the minute they said, 'I'd like to do Comedy Technique', I thought, 'You're not coming here.' Of course, there is such a thing as a sense of comedy.

Athene Seylor's book, *The Craft of Comedy*, is worth reading, but I rather suspect that it's only helpful to people who know something about being funny in the first place. I was taken to meet her when she was about 98. By the time I met her she didn't go out much and sat most of the time in her window in Chiswick. Children, everybody, knew her and waved as they passed. She said, 'That's a policewoman I'm very, very fond of—we always have a wave. I think, after a lot of consideration, I've decided not to become a policewoman. I'd be hopeless at

arresting people. I'd say, "Darling, please don't do it again.'"
Athene had been married to Nicholas Hannen—'Beau'
Hannen, as he was called, because he was so handsome and a
great dandy. She said, 'Of course, he died years and years and
years ago, and he's sitting up there going, "Where is she? What
is she doing?"'

She told me about seeing Henry Irving when she was a child:
'Don't ask me what he was like. He came on stage, and I
fainted.' Then the clock struck twelve and she broke off to say,
'It's rather an intrusive, noisy clock, but I think what it's saying
is, "Time for a drink." The sherry is over there.'

She was very witty and amusing—and she said something I
found interesting: 'I was cast as Madame Ranyevskaia. The first
thing Tyrone Guthrie said was, "And I don't want any Athene
Seylor tricks." I could hardly do the part after that.' Athene
was a terrific comic actress.

Lolly: What was it about her that was funny?

George: I don't know. What is it about any great performer?
It's all so fascinating and very mysterious. Isn't that what keeps
us interested? Edith Evans said: 'I didn't know what I wanted
to do, but I knew I wanted to do a job you'd never get to the
end of.'

Edith was very funny, too, but you never really knew if it
was deliberate or not. When Gwynneth Thurburn retired
as Principal from Central in 1967, Edith presided over the
occasion. She lightened the evening by dropping envelopes,
pretending confusion, and she made the whole thing
hysterically funny. It was quite an elaborate performance. Then
afterwards she said, 'I think that took the curse off.' And you
just weren't sure if she'd set the whole thing up.

Lolly: Who else has made you laugh?

George: Eric Morecambe was funny—in-built funny—and I think Les Dawson is funny. 'Funny bones' they call it in variety. Noël Coward makes me laugh. In the introduction to 'Piccolo Marina' he says, 'In the *nick*…of time.' And somehow he makes the word 'nick' funny. I remember seeing Lucille Ball doing the longest double take I'd ever seen in my life. I don't know, she saw a person inside a refrigerator or something, and she went away and did what seemed to be about ten things before it hit her. She managed to maintain a total absorption in what she was doing before that realisation hit her.

Among the people I've worked with, Bernard Cribbins made me laugh all the time. You could say to him, 'I bet you can't get a laugh on such and such a line'. And he would. He didn't do anything obvious like crossing his eyes—he could just get a laugh. I suppose some comedy is mastery of the sheer mechanics. The most brilliant analytical actor I ever worked with from that point of view was Stanley Baxter. He could say, 'If you put the cup down after the line, instead of on it, the laugh will come,' and it did.

Lolly: There are things like: 'If you say the line and then move, the emphasis is on the move. If you move and then say the line, the emphasis is on the line.'

George: But then, I think it's all mysteries, all paradoxes. Someone once said to George Abbot, 'You don't think there's only one way to do a line?' and he replied, 'There's only one best way.' That's pretty good. Yet you can often prove the opposite. I suppose no one knows exactly what it is, but I do know that some people just make me laugh. Have you ever seen Sheila Steafal? I think she has a touch of comic genius. She did an evening for a charity here in Brighton a few years ago and I thought that she was the funniest person I'd seen since Bea Lillie.

In the mid '50s I was at the Piccolo Theatre with Ann Morrish and Chrissie Hearne, and we went to see Lillie when she came to Manchester in *An Evening with Beatrice Lillie*. She was a legend and we were quite nervous that she wouldn't be up to her reputation. She walked on stage and the three of us screamed. And all she'd done was walk on stage!

From the account in the Coward diaries, she drove people insane in rehearsals—because she thought the material wasn't funny—and, of course, nobody knew if it *was* going to be funny. She'd be a nervous wreck, then she got in front of an audience and she was hysterical. Her comedy was so esoteric. Her jokes were so private and personal, that it's amazing they made anybody laugh.

Lolly: So if there is no such thing as comedy technique or the craft of comedy—or if you just have to be born with 'funny bones'—how can we mere mortals ever hope to get to a laugh?

George: Trying things, I suppose, but really there is no absolute answer. My friend Cilla Morgan was in the first production of *Separate Tables* and she had a line that got a huge laugh. One night, after about six months, they suddenly stopped laughing. The laugh didn't come back and everybody, *everybody*—even Terence Rattigan who'd written it—said, 'I think you used to do…'. After several months, the audience laughed again and they laughed for the rest of the run. There was some subtle thing, but what was it?

If you are very inexperienced and there is a line that always gets a laugh and one night the audience doesn't get it—or if there is a scene that always goes well and then one night they don't get it—you have to fight a feeling that that particular audience knew that everybody had laughed up to now and not only did they not laugh, they all got together before the show and *agreed* to not laugh.

I think one of the differences between plays and musicals is that if you lose the audience's interest in a play, it can be irretrievable. But you get to that point in a musical, then do a six- or seven-minute production number with very exciting orchestrations and terrific choreography, and you've got them again.

Lolly: Did you do musicals at the Vic?

George: Yes, and we had singing lessons, but the thing about the Vic was its huge emphasis on physical skills. Litz Pisk taught movement and she was wonderful. Her movement classes were a revelation. I'd been a terribly non-physical child. Hated games. Hated moving. Hated swimming. I developed a passion for swimming when I was in Bombay and Singapore, but I'd never really 'moved'. Litz's classes transformed my life. I was a stiff, fat, non-mover and within three weeks of starting the course I felt completely released. I was still quite fat, though, and Michel used to say things like, 'You are amazing when you dance, because I quite forget about your body.' Thanks! Very encouraging.

Lolly: I only worked with Litz once, in my third-year at Central, when she came for a week with Ronald Harwood and the BBC to film sections of *The Bacchae* for a series called *All the World's a Stage.*

George: There was a lot of wonderful work that week, but what we filmed was never in the show. We tried to trace it when Litz's exhibition was on at the National Theatre. It had all been wiped.

Lolly: I remember Litz's work that week as being very grounded, weighty, and centred very low.

George: But, you see, you were doing a very specific thing. When she was doing the minuet, it was all up and high. She had these peasant hands, and yet she'd do an elegant court dance, and they would become exquisite.

Lolly: Why was her teaching so special?

George: She had no ideal body she was aiming for. It was all about releasing and perfecting each student's own unique body. She felt that movement came from a centre and, as in musical transposition, there was something there that you just 'switched' to move into a different key, become a different person.

But I think one of the greatest things about Litz was her total lack of jargon. More and more I think that jargon is how people stop thinking. It seems these days that everybody has a name for every process, and the minute you do that you stop thinking. Jargon in drama training is unhelpful. When criticising students, I try to use language that anybody not in the business will understand. Often people feel the need to dress it up. Personally, I try to avoid even terms like 'subtext' or 'in the moment'. I'd rather find the exact words appropriate to every occasion. I was always impressed by Litz's ability to express in ordinary English the impression somebody had made on her. Everybody understood what Litz was talking about all the time.

I worked with Litz a lot over the years. We did show after show—for as long as she worked—and although the work was always very serious, there was something in our relationship that made me think of Laurel and Hardy. Any run-through of a play when I was feeling pleasantly relieved by the result, Litz would always say, 'Where is the flaw?' I could have killed her! She was the mistress of what I called 'the Viennese shrug', a physical manifestation of her disappointment in your low standards. Whereas she was a very self-critical perfectionist, the minute I thought it was all right, I would say, 'Great!' So she would sit me down: 'You're really happy about the music you've done?' 'Yes, I think am, Litz.' She'd shrug: 'You like that bar of

6/8 between…?' 'Yes, Litz, I do.' Another shrug: 'You really like it?' 'Yes, Litz.' Two smaller shrugs: silence. 'Yes, Litz, I was very happy with it.' Three tiny, tiny shrugs. Part of her skill in getting her way with me, with designers and with actors, was in how she bravely put up with her disappointment at how feeble our ideas were. It made us dig deeper and try harder.

Michael Elliott did *The Tempest* for Theatre 69 at the University Theatre, which is now the Contact Theatre, at the top of their second season. That was really the beginning of the Royal Exchange. Richard Negri's set was something like twenty tons of sand and my pleasing fantasy was that the hotel where we lived only pretended to believe us when we said we were off to rehearsal. They really thought that Litz and I were going to Blackpool every day—the showers were always full of sand. The University still had sand turning up years later. It was a wonderful production. Mickey Feast was an Ariel of genius. Stunning. And there were twelve guys, almost straight out of Central, playing the spirits. Those students were very much the product of Litz's training and mine: they'd done animals, group singing, all sorts of imaginative movement. We couldn't have found people anywhere else who had all had the same background. Litz would say, 'I want you to be spirits that transform into animals.' She'd be sad if people were less than wonderful and that sadness meant that everyone just got better. She didn't upbraid anybody; her sadness that our imagination was inadequate did the trick. She once said to this boy, 'I don't believe you're a dog; I just don't believe it!' So to prove he was, he bit a lump out of her skirt!

Lolly: She must have been quite young when she was teaching at the Vic School.

George: She was in her 30s, but until she got into the movement studio she seemed like quite an old lady. Her face was deeply lined; she had circles under her eyes. I think the strain of being an Austrian in this country during the war had a profound effect on her.

Lolly: Had she been a dancer?

George: As a child, she had a spine curvature and her parents took her to Isadora Duncan's sister, who was teaching dance in Vienna. Litz became wonderful at movement, but she knew she wanted to study design as well. To do both, she figured she had to work in the theatre, so when she was sixteen she got into the Reinhardt Seminar, which was Max Reinhardt's drama school in Austria. She came to England from Vienna very early in the 1930s when it became clear something was brewing with Hitler. She had a lot of introductions in London, so within a couple of weeks she got a job at the Evening Standard as a theatre cartoonist and immediately was sent out to cover all the first nights. She had to ask, 'Who is that?' and she'd be told, 'That's John Gielgud,' or 'That's Laurence Olivier.'

Then Sir Kenneth Barnes hired Litz to teach movement at RADA. Like all the schools at the time, RADA only did ballet classes—really not much use for actors—and there were classes in deportment taught by Dame Irene Vanbrugh, Sir Kenneth's sister, that largely consisted of young women walking about with books on their heads and learning how to pour tea gracefully.

Sir Kenneth was wonderful to Litz—he helped her get her citizenship and he thought what she was doing was interesting—but he drew the line when she suggested classes in improvisation, which wasn't done at all in the '30s. Harold Lang, Alan Badell and Miriam Brickman, who were students at the time, all became Litz's passionate devotees, and these kids paid for a rehearsal room so that she'd do improvisation with them. Litz was an inspiring teacher. I know I couldn't have survived the Old Vic without her.

"The Old Vic Theatre School training was very hard, very tough. You started off as a quite confident and unselfconscious amateur, doing your audition, hopefully getting them to notice good things about you; but the purpose of the school was to make you aware of what had to be put right, all your terrible faults. That could be very depressing. So you went into what they called 'the tunnel', and if you were lucky you began to see the light at the end of that tunnel. It could be destructive on people who were vulnerable, and there was a small percentage of people who thought, 'In that case, I'm not going to go on with it.' I remember doing some part in a student show and everybody thought it was successful. I was walking down the corridor and Michel stopped me and said: 'You are out of the tunnel. Can you remember what you did and can you do it again?' And I thought, 'That nearly sends me back into the tunnel!' George Devine later tapped me on the shoulder and said, 'There you are, you see?' That was the difference between those two mentors at the Old Vic School."

Dame Joan Plowright, DBE, The Lady Olivier

Lolly: So your two great influences at the Vic were Percy Harris and Litz Pisk.

George: And the brilliant Suria Magito. I loved working with her. She had a wonderful way of implying that problems would solve themselves—'It's not very good today; I'm sure it will be beautiful tomorrow'—yet every time she directed a show, Michel or Glen Byam Shaw took it over to 'save' it. The men, well, they weren't misogynist by any means, but they could only think of Suria as a teacher and not a director, and they certainly didn't give her the respect she deserved in that sphere. I was in a little Offenbach operetta toward the end of my training, which Suria was doing beautifully. Michel came to see it, and for the next three days he took it over and it got worse. Then Suria came back and it got better again.

She and Michel had an affair and later married. When Michel was still with his first wife, his family used to call Suria 'la Situation'. Really, she was incredibly sophisticated and was the sole source of glamour in the school. When I first knew her, she had jet-black hair with that Diaghilev long white streak; and she was always so wonderfully turned out, impeccable from morning to night. She bought a suit from Dior every year, wore it every day and it looked a million dollars. She had a stiff scarf that she tied in a bow and it stayed there all day. No one could figure out how she did that. She was devastatingly stylish.

Lolly: When Saint-Denis began a new year, he or one of the other directors would direct a Shakespeare play—what they called 'The Test'—the idea being to throw students in at the deep end to see their strengths and weaknesses. Do you remember your 'Test'?

George: Yes, Glen Byam Shaw directed *Much Ado About Nothing*, which we did in three weeks. Of course the result was a mess, but they were delighted because they thought the mess told them where to go with us. Then in the first term we did a play. Immediately. I still think that is the way to do it: start work on a play immediately.

But I think the most profoundly important thing about the Vic training under Michel was the vision of making acting, voice and movement non-compartmentalized. That changed training everywhere; it had just never been done like that. The existence of the Vic School challenged all the other drama schools in existence at that time. They all had to adapt, in some way, to a new and interesting force. It became the norm for all British drama schools—all English-speaking drama schools.

Yet I think there were certainly things wrong with it. I played Pishchik in *The Cherry Orchard*, and Michel said, 'That's not how the role was done at the Moscow Arts Theatre.' I thought, 'But that's not the way you *tell* us to work!'

I think mostly people who were directed by Michel didn't feel great freedom. Gielgud was wary of him, Olivier was wary of him; and although they did some of their best work for him, I think they felt a sense of confinement. I remember a sweet but naïve boy at the Vic who was playing a servant in *The Clandestine Marriage*. His way in to the character was to say, 'It's sort of an Arthur Treacher part?' George Devine said,

'That's not the way we work.' They didn't recognise, that when you are struggling, anything at all is a lifeline.

In one of his books Michel said, 'I've been accused of being sadistic.' Of course he wasn't at all sadistic, but he was a severe taskmaster. The crit sessions at the end of term were unendurable—they would start at 9 AM and could go on until 10 PM. I suppose his behaviour was the result of a misplaced idealism, but really, Michel said some dreadful things to people. I remember there was a very large girl in my group and after a play presentation he said, 'You walk on stage, I ask myself: Is it a girl? Is it a horse?'

The other thing they often said in crits—and spot the flaw in the logic—'What you did didn't come off, but you worked in the right way.' I can remember thinking, 'If it was the right way, it'd come off: and if it didn't come off, it couldn't be the right way.'

I feel like half of what I later did as a teacher was indebted to the Vic and the other half was in reaction to it. The work at the school was remarkable: I totally accepted it and I think I took it with me to Central when I taught there. What I didn't take was the atmosphere, which I think was crippling. The great flaw of the place was that they didn't understand the word 'encouragement'—the word hadn't ever occurred to anybody— so one's first terrible nursery efforts were given criticisms that were crippling. What I inherited from the Vic was a great sense of the value of the training—and a great desire never to behave like that. I know I have worked always in accordance with the aims and always in reaction against the atmosphere.

For a lot of people, the last crits of their training were: 'You still cannot bring the text off the page.' It was an unhelpful parting gift for students as they stepped out into the professional theatre. My last crit was very poor and I remember getting on the bus and crying non-stop all the way to Camden Town.

Then a week later I got a phone call asking if I could come and see Michel. Litz was leaving to work in the visual arts, teaching movement to painters, and Michel offered me her job as dance teacher. I turned him down, but that day Michel said to me, 'You will always have an untidy career, but you could well become a complete man of the theatre.' I thought, 'If you'd only told me that a week ago!'

If we hadn't had that further conversation, I'm not sure I'd have gone on with it.

Lolly: How long did the Old Vic School exist?

George: Having started in 1946, very much with the blessing of the Labour government, in 1952 there was a falling out with the Arts Council and a lot of weird things with Tyrone Guthrie, and the place closed. The demise of the Vic School formed a lot of enemies. An Arts Council officer was quoted as saying, 'I found it so demeaning to see these students being animals and scuttling around on the floor.' And when the school was closed, appalling things happened. Students complained to the governors and Lady Violet Bonham Carter said something like, 'I'm prepared to talk to any member of the staff who is A) a qualified teacher and B) British.' In the atmosphere of the time there was an unspoken distrust in the fact that Michel was French, Litz a Viennese, Jani a Hungarian and Suria a Russian. In a better world than this, we could have been celebrating 60 years of the Vic School, rather than remembering its six years. Fewer and fewer people even know it ever existed.

Nevertheless, it was extremely important to post-war British theatre. A number of people who trained with Michel went on to become teachers and the Vic School became the prototype for modern training. It had a huge effect.

I wouldn't have missed the Vic, yet I found it desperately inhibiting. A lot of people found it difficult to make the adjustment to the profession when they got out. Prunella Scales said it was only when she was in New York with *The Matchmaker* and went to Uta Hagan that she started to sort it out. I could act not badly when I went, I couldn't act very well at all when I left, and it took me five or six years struggling in rep in the early '50s to get away from the training and relax. Curiously enough, I felt totally at home when I was doing cabaret.

When I left the school I immediately got two jobs at once—a situation that must seem incredible to today's students. I did a revue at a place called the Watergate Theatre, which was in Of Alley near Charing Cross Station. They've changed the name of the street to something else now and I am so irritated with them. The naming of the streets in that district was so witty. They were all called after George Villiers, Duke of whatever, so there was George Street, Villiers Street, Duke Street and, most amusingly, Of Alley. Now they've changed it to something mundane. Maddening.

Anyway, I was in *Let's Do a Revue* there with Joan Plowright, Margaret Ashcroft (Peggy's niece, who had been in my year at the Vic), Elizabeth Thorndike who was Dame Sybil Thorndike's niece, and Christopher Hancock. Christopher Hewitt, who had been in all the Hermione Gingold shows, devised the revue and I wrote music and lyrics. Simultaneously, I went into the Old Vic Company to do *Tambourlaine the Great*. I moved into a room just by the Cambridge Theatre and I could walk to the Watergate and I could walk to the Old Vic. I thought that was the most glamorous thing in the world.

Tambourlaine the Great was a fabulous production directed by Tyrone Guthrie and starring Donald Wolfit. I was an assistant stage manager and played small parts, but I also understudied Leo McKern: he had one big part, which somebody else had covered, and I covered his smaller, comic part. Terrifyingly, on the second night he was ill! Even more frightening was one of

Guthrie's striking ideas: in one scene, we were shot at and I had to fall just beside this hole on the stage and one of the soldiers contemptuously would push me away with his foot until I fell down the hole where people were waiting to catch me. It was a long time before the push and I used to lie there thinking, 'What if those 'catchers' are not there?' I can wake up in the night even now and feel nervous about it.

Lolly: What was Tyrone Guthrie like?

George: Fantastic! He was very tall and military looking with a little clipped moustache, and he had a wife who was as big as he was. In memory, they seem seven feet tall. And they brought their terrible looking sandwiches in a brown paper bag for their lunches. Guthrie didn't want to be smart, didn't want to be 'West End', was absolutely the antithesis of the 'smart theatre'. Guthrie would rather do something for four pence in the West Highlands of Scotland than do anything commercial. When he did the first production of Bernstein's *Candide*, I played for some of the auditions and I remember he said, 'This is either going to be world-shaking or it will be the most pretentious piece of nonsense you've ever seen in your life.' It never seemed to bother him what the response was from the critics. He just didn't care. He was fearless.

He was a little crazy, too. Leslie Hurry had designed these little loincloth things for *Tamburlaine*. Guthrie said, 'Oh, they're far too big,' and he enthusiastically got the scissors and came along and trimmed our loincloths. And he spoke in telegrams. 'Well done!' That's all you got. I've never forgotten this: Leo McKern came in and said, 'Tony, I'm terribly sorry I'm late, but I had to go and have a wig fitting,' and Guthrie said, 'Well understood. Needful to be done.' But he made actors feel totally free—you could do anything at a Guthrie rehearsal. He encouraged it. 'Do something different.' If you lay on the floor, he'd go, 'Well, maybe.'

He loved small part actors, so if one of us smaller part people came up with a ridiculous gag, Guthrie encouraged us; but he didn't really like stars, so could be incredibly naughty. Donald Wolfit had been an actor-manager, so it was the first time in about fifteen years he hadn't been his own director. Everybody was waiting to see how these two giants were going to react to each other, and Guthrie would give notes like, 'Donald, act two. Verse speaking, atrocious!' You couldn't believe it was happening.

Lolly: Was Wolfit like he was portrayed in Ronald Harwood's *The Dresser?*

George: I must say he had great power, but for me the strokes were too bold and I saw little or no subtlety. Ronnie had a great regard for him, but I found him less attractive. I once saw him in the wings take a whole mouthful of grapes and spit pips everywhere. As the assistant stage manager, I had to take personal props back to him, and on one occasion he had his feet in a basin of water and his poor downtrodden wife was washing them. Guthrie gave Wolfit quite a tough time. At one point he accused him of acting in an undemocratic way towards the company, so Wolfit started being hideously, transparently unctuous: 'Good morning. Do you know my wife, Rosalind Iden?' The plan had been for Wolfit to do a whole series of plays at the Vic, but he was plainly uncomfortable and withdrew.

After *Tambourlaine* and the revue, I spent most of 1952 in music hall, which was by that time called variety. Mike Morgan had been at the Vic and we made each other laugh from the moment we met, so we put together a double act called 'The Country Cousins'. We did a song, some patter, then we did another song. Mike's sister, Priscilla Morgan—Cilla—joined the act later.

If we had been Picasso in his early years or Martha Graham in her first weeks of performing, we couldn't have hit such a wall of hostility and confusion. Nobody knew why Mike and I were dressed up as such old men. Agents were totally mystified. They said, 'But you're young…? You're quite good-looking…?' I wrote a song called 'Manure', which sounds harmless now, but it made hardened agents go pale. When we were on the road, we met a husband and wife team who had been with Fred Karno's Army—the group of touring music hall artists where Chaplin and Stan Laurel started. This elderly couple understood our intentions, but they still thought we didn't have a hope in hell!

I had this huge padding—it was as if we were staging a revolt against the smooth new comedians in their well-cut suits. One night we did two shows at the Grand in Walham Green and then we had a show at the Nuffield Centre near St. Martin-in-the-Fields so, still in our costumes, we went by cab with our huge prop stile. I remember thinking, 'If there is a car-crash, what will they think at the hospital when all our stuffing comes out?' The wigs and makeup took about an hour and a half and the act was only ten minutes long—very 'Vic School' in a way. At that time actors used makeup as disguise: you felt that if you went to a costume parade and people knew who you were you had failed. I didn't have my own nose in the theatre for about three and a half years. It was all goatees and glue and nose putty.

Lolly: What happened to Mike Morgan?

George: He was a brilliant actor and his first job after the Vic was to play the boy in *Henry V* at Stratford. We did our year in variety and some rep, then he did a movie with Alec Guinness called *Barnacle Bill*—Guinness thought he was wonderful. Then, in 1958 during his next film, *The Horse's Mouth,* Mike

"The West of England company toured out of Exmouth. We had very short rehearsal periods and then travelled around to small towns in Devon to play for one night, where they were very pleased to see us, I might add. We played in a church hall or a slaughterhouse and there were no wings, so you often had to go out of the side door and around the back of the hall to get in the other side of the set. The actors went on a bus, the set would come in a truck, and you'd get your costume out of a big hamper and iron it yourself, do the show, then pack it all up and go back to the base."

Dame Joan Plowright, DBE, The Lady Olivier

died of meningitis. He was going to have a great, great career. Such a shame. A sadness.

Lolly: You went into rep after 'Country Cousins'?

George: I spent 1953 in the West of England Company, but really that was never like being in an ordinary rep because everybody was going somewhere. It had Joan Plowright, Phyllida Law, Avril Elgar, Eric Thompson, Rosalind Knight, Annie Leake and David Terence. Clare Jeffery was the designer. All Vic students.

In 1954, Richard Negri, who had been a design student at the Vic, had just finished two years at Oldham Coliseum; and he and Frank Dunlop started a company called the Piccolo Players.

At the Vic we had been encouraged to change the theatre—over-encouraged perhaps—but it did mean that people were quite daring about what they did. The company had Mike Morgan, Casper Wrede from the Vic directing course, Clare Jeffery from the design course, Eric Thompson, Rosalind Knight, June Brown, Cilla Morgan, Avril Elgar, Dilys Hamlett, John Roberts, Lee Montague, Phyllida Law, Ida Goldapple and Bernard Cribbins. Many of those people, in effect, went on to run the Exchange Theatre in Manchester. It was almost entirely Vic people—Bernard Cribbins was a notable exception.

The theatre was in the upper floor of the Conservative Club in Chorlton-cum-Hardy, a suburb of Manchester. Richard Negri did most of the designing, and he had an assistant, Dorothy Marshall. We literally, with our own hands, turned this upstairs room into a 200-seat theatre, with a forestage jutting out from the proscenium. Richard found out that the cheapest material in the world was the white shrouding that you wrapped corpses in, so he draped acres of it over this hideous vaulted and beamed ceiling, and Dorothy painted a mile of black stripes on it. They hung little chandeliers. It was beautiful. Peggy Ashcroft came to open it; Sybil Thorndike, Lewis Casson, Glen Byam Shaw and Michel became patrons.

The newspapers would slate things at the Manchester Opera House or the Grand, but they fell in love with us. The first season opened with *The Women Have Their Way* by the Brothers Quintero, and we did *Arsenic and Old Lace, The Taming of the Shrew,* and *She Stoops to Conquer,* which was set in the wilds of Ireland. I played Hardcastle, Rosalind Knight was Mrs. Hardcastle and Bernard Cribbins played Digory. Richard and Frank had decided they wanted to do the melodrama *Maria Marten, or Murder in the Red Barn* as a musical, so I wrote all the songs in a couple of weeks, then I played the piano, decided the keys—and for the first time really started to direct people on how to perform songs.

The second season ran from October '54 to January '55. James Maxwell joined the company—he was an American who trained at the Vic with Ann Morrish, Patrick Wymark and Margaret Ashcroft. George Devine guest directed a production of Goldoni's *Mirandolina*, designed by Joceyln Herbert. But even though the critics loved us we ran out of money, so it only lasted a spring and an autumn season.

Between the two seasons, we did a play called *Mary Stuart* at the Edinburgh Festival. It was a dreadful play by a Corsican called Joseph Chiari, but he was willing to fund it so we found a disused church in the Pleasance to do it in. When we went to reconnoitre the space, we realised there was this church hall in the back, so Phyllida Law and I raised £30 and I wrote twenty numbers for a late night revue called *The Green Room Show.*

Every offstage moment in *Mary Stuart* was spent preparing snacks, which we sold just before the revue started. It was all great fun. Richard Negri designed it; and the company was drawn from the cast of *Mary Stuart*—with the exceptions of a marvellous woman called Annie Leake, and Roger Gage, who was then Joan Plowright's husband.

At the same time in the Festival there was an Oxford University Drama Society production of *Edward II* directed by Casper Wrede. OUDS had always been a great entrée to the theatre, and Casper had been a professional guest director for a couple of their shows. His assistant was Michael Elliott, who had just graduated from Oxford; his designer was Malcolm Pride from the Vic; James Maxwell played the lead and Dilys Hamlett played opposite him. And they did one of the first Oxford revues at the Festival with a cast that included Maggie Smith—who was already scintillating, brilliant beyond belief, despite her youth. There was very little Fringe then—it was in its infancy—and there were only about four or five late night revues that year, so our two companies got to know each other very well.

Almost immediately after that, Michael Elliott became a hugely successful TV director and he used all those same people all the time. They were the people he knew, and he didn't know many people. I always said Michael went to the Vic by osmosis—he missed all the pain, but got all the rewards.

Lolly: What did you do after the second Piccolo season finished?

George: That Christmas I wrote the music and lyrics for *Aladdin* at the Queen's Theatre, Hornchurch. Stuart Burge wrote and directed it, Joan Plowright played Itti Sing and Bernard Cribbins played Bobbil. That group from the Piccolo all went their separate ways but those connections remained very tight, so when Frank Dunlop became the director of the '55 season at the Midland Theatre Company in Coventry, he hired me.

That company had Sheila Ballantyne, Rosalind Knight, Eric Thompson—and Alan Bates in his first job out of RADA. Alan played Antipholus of Ephesus and I played Balthazar in *The Comedy of Errors*—he was the young lead in *You and Your Wife* and I played Bowles. Then we did *The Lark* and *The Matchmaker*, where I played Malachi Stack and he played one of the waiters.

I loved Alan! He was just lovely, and so very, very funny. When he was young, two subjects dominated his conversation: his spots and his constipation. At my retirement at the Duke of York's, he did that Tom Stoppard piece—I think Stoppard wrote it for him—where he came on with a lot of Shakespeare pieces and dropped them and did a muddled version of Shakespeare. He was a wonderful madman. He did twelve different Simon Grey scripts on stage and TV: he understood confused characters so well. When he was at RADA and just after, he lived in a house in Battersea that had at various times Albert Finney, Brian Bedford and Keith Baxter. It was an infamous house, up to no good. Six months out of RADA, Alan was playing Cliff in *Look Back in Anger* at the Royal Court and I don't think he was ever out of work again. We remained close for a number of years.

Lolly: You kept up with a lot of the people you worked with in those early days of your career.

George: We kept working with one another. For years. Everyone went away and had successes separately, but we also worked together when we could.

Lolly: It was around this time that you co-directed *Jubilee Girl* with Casper Wrede?

George: That was so odd. In the spring of 1956, I got this very strange phone call. There were two doctors, Robin Fordyce and David Rogers—and one of them had married an heiress so they had money to burn. They were really amateur writers and their show, *Jubilee Girl*, went around England changing directors just about every Thursday—they'd got through about twenty people.

I had just come from the labour exchange, and I got a call to meet these two doctor-writers in Chester Square, so I darted down there straight from the dole to have the door opened by a butler and be ushered in for some very grand drinks. And they asked if Casper and I would be interested in co-directing *Jubilee Girl* for the Victoria Palace.

They described the show and we said we'd have to see it before we decided. Curiously enough, the company was on a paid week of not performing, so the cast was all summoned to do the show for us one afternoon at the Garrick. The Garrick had a show on called *La Plume de Ma Tante* with Robert Dhery—it was a brilliant, semi-slapstick but very sophisticated French revue—I'd seen it several times and I adored it—and there was this wonderful, totally unexplained bit, where a man wearing a cape and southwester sat on a horse and sang a song about Devon. And the horse yawned. It was glorious. Well, the show was going to be on that night at the theatre and the horse couldn't get through this very difficult stage door, so it was brought through the theatre auditorium and taken backstage through the pass door. So Casper and I were sitting alone in this theatre, like Ludvig, the mad King of Bavaria, watching thirty people perform for us and thinking 'this show is crap'— and suddenly this man leads a horse down the centre aisle and through the pass door. Isn't that bizarre?

I had great fun. I'm appalled now when I realise we were nobody and in our short careers had earned tuppence, and yet

we said things like, 'Every costume in that scene has to go.'
Gasp: 'But that will cost £30,000!' We sat them down and
told them their show was muddled, helped them to get a better
story line, and rewrote a lot of the lyrics and music. I knew
I might never have that kind of chance again, so I asked for a
publicity budget to experiment with ways of advertising. At
that time, sandwich board people were all decrepit old men, so
I got all my best-looking friends to do the sandwich boards. I
found that one of our dressers, a funny old woman who lived
in Chelsea, came to the theatre by pony and trap instead of by
bus, so I covered the sides of the trap with advertising for the
show. Whether or not any of it had any effect, I have no idea.

Lolly: How long did it run?

George: It did six weeks of twice nightly and it did a lot better
than it would have if Casper and I hadn't been involved. Really,
it could only have a short run anyway. Jack Hilton had quite
cynically engineered it to give the Crazy Gang a holiday, but
every lunchtime the Crazy Gang, far from rushing to warm
climes for a rest, popped into the pub next door to the theatre.
That was one of the great joys of that job.

Casper and I worked together again a number of times over
the years and I wrote the music for two of his first films: *The
Barber of Stamford Hill* and *Private Potter*, both of which were
written by Ronald Harwood. *Private Potter*, which starred Tom
Courtney, has recently played somewhere—probably at 2AM
on a wet Thursday in Kansas—because I got a tiny royalty
cheque.

Lolly: Were they the only two films you did?

George: As a composer, yes. I appeared briefly in *All for Mary*,
directed by Wendy Toye, and I did the craziest job for Alfred
Shaughnessey—who later wrote *Upstairs, Downstairs*. At that
time, you could get some generalized music from Chapels—

written by some hack composer—and not pay royalties for it. So they gave me something that was like a march, to which I put a melody line and a lyric. It was filmed in the Metropolitan, a famous old music hall on the Edgeware Road, and I think I was seen as a shadowy figure, conducting this hack music.

Then from the end of '55 until the early '60s, I did a lot of incidental music for Casper's and Michael Elliott's shows at the BBC. Either together, or sometimes Michael on his own, they did things like *The Lady from the Sea* and *Uncle Vanya*. Can you imagine that happening today? We did a production of *The Women of Troy*, for which Litz did the movement and I did the sound. I did music for a lovely production of *She Stoops to Conquer* with Ralph Richardson and Tom Courtney.

My very first was an obscure Tennessee Williams piece called *You Touched Me*, which was based on a short story by D. H. Lawrence, and had the great Wilfred Lawson and Fay Compton, with Avril Elgar playing one of her early television roles. It was live and I played the incidental music. I had found a broken barrel organ at Television Centre and I liked the sound of it, but it was difficult because the piano's bass to treble is left to right and a barrel organ bass to treble goes the other way. So I made charts and had to mark the organ with numbers, then I wrote out the score with numbers—1, 3, 7, 5—and played it that way.

I still did the odd role here and there, too. When Michael and Casper did *Twelfth Night* for the BBC, I did the music and was cast as Fabian. David Terence was Valentine and Cilla Morgan was Maria. James Maxwell was Feste, Dilys was Viola, Maureen Quinney was Olivia, Eric Thompson was Antonio. All the same people again.

It's now unimaginable, but in the '50s at the BBC when Michael had done a play, he didn't do another until the spirit moved him. He went into the office and read scripts, then he'd suddenly go to Michael Barrie, who was the Head of Drama, and say, 'I'd like to do *Uncle Vanya*.' So one day I went to Barrie and said, 'Michael and I would like to do a musical, which I'll write,' and he said, 'Alright, I'll commission you.' Just like that. It was a different world. So I did *Sing for Your Supper*, which I believe was the first musical that had ever been especially devised for television. Cilla Morgan and John Hewer were the leads; and it had Lally Bowers and Maggie Smith.

Then, in 1958, I got a series called *Better Late* and became a Music Associate for BBC Light Entertainment. That was a curious show. Duncan MacRae, very cherished by Tyrone Guthrie, was an eccentric, almost grotesque, Scottish actor who gave a strong, strong colour to everything. At the time, it was the most bizarre thing in the world for him to front this show with his heavy Scottish accent. Two very young dancers in the show were Una Stubbs and Amanda Barrie.

At last I was being properly paid and I started to pay off debts. Then in 1959 and '60, I did a series that was much better paid still. *On the Bright Side*, starring Stanley Baxter and Betty Marsden, was an enormous success. In those days there weren't all the channels there are today and they went out live, so it was very exciting to know that a huge proportion of the population would be watching. There was an immediacy that television now lacks, when there are so many channels to watch and one can record anything and watch it whenever. The show went out fortnightly and the next morning one heard reactions from across the country. As well as having two great comic talents, the musical side was very strong indeed with Pip Hinton, Eira Heath and David Kernan. We took enormous care about choosing and rehearsing the songs. We had two notable choreographers: Alfred Rodrigues in the first series and Douglas Squires in the second; and again, dancers Una Stubbs and Amanda Barrie.

After *On the Bright Side*, there was a stage version called *On the Brighter Side* at the Phoenix Theatre, and I wrote material for that, too. We added to the principal cast: Ronnie Barker had done some of the shows for the BBC, and Judy Carne, who went on to do *Rowan and Martin's Laugh-In* for American TV.

And all during that time I also worked on some 'TV spectaculars'—glorified variety shows, really—with people like Katherine Grayson and Jeannie Carson, who were big names then.

Lolly: From very early on, you were being hired for your musical skills. Did that seduce you away from acting?

George: By the end of the '50s, the music was becoming predominant. Then Michel Saint-Denis got in touch with me again. He'd been asked to design a curriculum for the National Theatre School of Canada and he asked me to go be in charge of movement. I was doing *On the Bright Side*, so I flew to Paris on a Friday and stayed the weekend in this little cottage in the country with Michel and Suria. I got to know him better that weekend than I ever had and his offer was tempting, but I didn't do it. I was getting into the whole musical and revue scene.

Lolly: And you were still doing theatre.

George: Yes. In 1959 Casper Wrede and Michael Elliott formed the 59 Theatre Company and took a lease on the Lyric Theatre, Hammersmith, to do a five-play season. A rich businessman backed it. Richard Negri, Malcolm Pride and Clare Jeffery were the designers. Richard Pilbrow, who was just up-and-coming, became the lighting designer; Litz did movement and I did the music.

The acting company again included a lot of the Vic's ex-students, but the group grew. Casper Wrede was Finnish and because he knew Michael Meyer from his Scandinavian times, they assimilated him—Michael had trained at the Old Vic as a director. Ronald Harwood not only joined the company as an actor, but he also became part of the inner group. That's where he really started writing. We did a play by someone in the company and I think Ronnie thought, 'If *he* can write a play, *I* can!'

Theatre 59 was a bit of a sensation. We did *Danton's Death*, with Avril Elgar playing Julie. Casper Wrede directed Strindberg's *The Creditors*, starring Mai Zetterling. Peter Dews directed the Ottway adaptation of Moliere's *The Cheats of Scapin*.

In the spring we did Ibsen's *Brand*, which was virtually the first production of it in this country. Everybody had thought *Brand* was a non-play, unstageable, really just a long dramatic poem. When this production opened, it made careers overnight. Patrick McGoohan was the lead, and the next day he woke up to find he was famous. It was Michael Elliott's breakthrough—he'd only done TV and never done anything in the theatre. It was Michael Meyer's breakthrough as a translator. At the end of the play there is an avalanche and the two Richards—Negri and Pilbrow—created a combination of light and sound that was a coup de théâtre. Richard Negri became a star designer; Richard Pilbrow started a huge career as a lighting designer. Nevertheless, in spite of the acclaim, the whole season lost money and again the company disbanded.

Then, in 1961 Michael Elliott was asked to do *As You Like It* for the Shakespeare Festival Theatre in Stratford, and so a lot of the group came together again. The management was greatly uncertain as to whether Rosalind would be Dorothy Tutin or Vanessa Redgrave—and I can tell you, it was a close thing! Vanessa gave a stunning performance. Richard Negri's set had a great feeling of open space and the outdoors. Litz did the dance and movement, and I wrote the music. In what was an otherwise lacklustre season, it was a huge success. After its run in Stratford, they brought it into the Aldwych in London, which was where they brought the Stratford successes then, and during its run there, half the cast had to leave to start the next Stratford season. Michael was doing a John Mortimer play out of town, so I re-directed *As You Like It* with the newcomers—a thrilling opportunity.

But I have to tell you, the most curious thing happened in 1961. Very, very strange. We'd all had our various successes and our careers had all got so far, but Michael and Casper— particularly Casper—thought we should have philosophical fortnightly meetings to discuss where we thought the theatre should be going, our function in it, what the theatres should look like, etc, etc. So we all got together for these fortnightly musings in somebody's flat or other: Ronnie Harwood, James Maxwell, Richard Negri, Malcolm Pride, Casper, Michael, myself. 'Where is the theatre going?' 'What should we collectively do?' We had these rather intense, voluble evenings. By that time Richard Negri was running the Theatre Design School at Wimbledon School of Art. Malcolm Pride became Richard's successor, but at that time was a very successful West End designer. Malcolm couldn't bear those meetings. He used to drink far too much—well, more than the rest of us anyway! Through Casper, we co-opted this amazing Finnish man called Amund Høningstadt, who was a philosopher and who totally, profoundly, understood Ibsen. I was told he used to sit in a café in Helsinki, and people came and bought him drinks and asked him questions. He would sip increasing amounts of whisky and tell them what their lives would be. At one of these meetings he said to me, 'You are the ecstatic one. You are the singer. You are the one who will work with the young.' Weird. At that time it really hadn't entered my mind that that would be what I'd end up doing.

Anyway, at one of these meetings we decided we'd had enough of the abstractions. In our arrogant way we had thrashed out what we thought the basis of the theatre should be and thought we now should do something more practical—'Let's say we are offered the Old Vic Theatre for a year. What would the repertoire be?' So we all brought our suggestions. At the end of that meeting, we had come up with our perfect season: 'Michael Meyer will do a new translation of *Peer Gynt*. Leo McKern is ideal casting and Richard will design it. We'll do *Othello*, which Casper will direct and Malcolm Pride will design, and we'll get the Danish actor, Moegens Veith. Wouldn't it be great to get Guthrie back to do a show? Wouldn't it be great to do what the theatre never does, which is to have a permanent movement teacher and a permanent voice teacher?' We thought we should have, in Granville-Barker's phrase, 'an exemplary theatre'. Then, within a week, Michael Elliott had a phone call from the Old Vic asking if he would take it over for its final year before Olivier brought in the National Theatre. Bizarre. It was already all set out!

So, in 1962, we all went to the Old Vic and had a year running the theatre. We did *Peer Gynt*. We did *Othello*. Sadly, Moegens, who'd been in *Private Potter* for Casper, died during rehearsals, but we got a wonderful West Indian actor called Errol John. It was an extraordinary year. I was resident composer and voice coach. Litz was choreographer and movement coach. I gave voice and singing tutorials to the company; she gave movement classes. You have to remember that although it's commonplace now for a company to have a dedicated voice and movement team, there was nobody doing that kind of work then.

Lolly: Was this your first experience in teaching, other than as a student at Heriot's?

George: I'd always taught music here and there; I'd done supply teaching after the war, waiting to go to the Vic. And in 1960, I'd started teaching at Toynbee Hall in the East End. Bertha

"I was one of the very lucky ones. To get into the Central School and be nurtured by the brilliant George Hall. This 'nurturing' not only consisted of trying to make us the best actors we could possibly be, but also to prepare us for the tricky life ahead. He drummed it into us that we would have a lot of time on our hands. That we would probably be more out of work than in. And even when employed there would be endless 'hanging about' in green rooms, film and TV studios waiting to go on and do your bit, so don't moan about it, occupy yourself. I never forgot this advice and during the longueurs of filming managed to complete a memoir and a novel. I shall be eternally grateful to him on how not to waste time."

Roberta Taylor, Actress, writer

Myers, who had been one of the junior tutors at the Vic School, was running evening classes at Toynbee for the Inner London Education Authority. Bertha was terribly austere. When we were at the Vic, Casper Wrede and Dilys Hamlett went off and got married one day in their lunch hour. When they came back and said, 'Bertha, we just got married!' she replied, 'Don't let it interfere with your work.'

Anyway, Toynbee Hall was more than just 'evening classes'. It had really become a very good drama school for people who couldn't afford to go to any of the fulltime drama schools—in fact, Roberta Taylor had been there before she came to audition for us at Central in the '70s.

Lolly: And Robbie's had a very successful career.

George: Yes, years of terrific theatre, then *Eastenders*, *The Bill*, and now she's a successful writer as well. Extraordinary.

Lolly: What did you teach at Toynbee Hall?

George: That was when I started teaching students about the history of musical theatre. It was a terrific preparation, as though I knew I'd needed that apprenticeship, and so by the time I went to Central in '63, I was an experienced teacher.

Lolly: Did you continue to work in the profession after you took over at Central?

George: Oh, yes, and I can't believe anyone who has been involved with training actors at a serious level has had as many absurd jobs as I have! I did *Sunday Night at the Palladium*, which was a big variety show every week for the BBC, and I played the piano while this man walked across the top of it on his hands, until finally his legs were drooping over my head. I can't think how that came about—perhaps I was already working in the show with Nina and Frederik.

Lolly: Should I know 'Nina and Frederik'?

George: If you'd been in England at that time, you couldn't have helped knowing them. Nina and Frederik were a very popular folk song cabaret act and they did masses of television in the '60s. They were extraordinarily beautiful, very popular.

Nina's father had been a movie director in Denmark; Frederik was Baron van Pallandt of Holland. They'd been childhood friends and had always sung together. Well, they were in some restaurant in Denmark and they sang, cameras were there, it was shown, and suddenly all Denmark wanted a record of them. They instantly became headliners, without any training or background.

When they wanted to broaden their style, Casper Wrede introduced them to me and I persuaded them do new material. I staged numbers, did rewrites and arrangements. Frederik was a fantastic linguist and had a wonderful ear, so we did things like 'Baby, It's Cold Outside' in American and then French, then as a very upper-crust Englishman. In the late '60s, I staged the summer show they did at the Dome in Brighton. We did a two-hour show at the Albert Hall and Talk of the Town.

We recorded an album at one point and for some reason they were an item short. I'd written a pavane for *Othello* at the Old Vic, which I'd adapted for a show at Central, so I hastily adapted it again for the two of them. Because it sounded both Elizabethan and modern, the publisher insisted on calling it

'Elizabeth One and Two'. Joe Loss's dance band ended up doing a version of it and I still get royalties.

The whole thing with Nina and Frederik could often get very bizarre. At one point I went to work with them in Ibiza at their Moorish farmhouse—they had bought it ten years earlier when Ibiza was a hippie commune and had about four cars and one road. By the time I was there it had all changed. Denholm Elliot had a place; Kenneth MacMillan, the choreographer, and Lynn Seymour, the dancer, went there a lot. It was there I had my two brushes with big international crime. I met a very nice man called Elmyr de Hory, who turned out to be a huge international art forger, and I have a hazy memory of meeting Clifford Irving, who seemed very nice. I didn't know until many years later that he was having an affair with Nina. He wrote the famous hoax autobiography of Howard Hughes and got caught because during one period of time that he claimed he'd been interviewing Hughes, Nina insisted Irving had been with her in Mexico. Big scandal: big news. He was shipped off to jail for that.

Lolly: What happened to Nina and Frederik?

George: They separated and Nina went to work in Hollywood, where she acted in films. Frederik was murdered in what was supposedly a very big drug-smuggling incident. The Nina and Frederik saga was quite extraordinary.

Lolly: While we're on 'what happened to'—what happened to all those people from the Piccolo and Theatre 59?

George: Casper moved into films. He and Ronnie Harwood wrote *The Barber of Stamford Hill* and *Private Potter*, and they worked together again on *A Day in the Life of Ivan Denisovich*. Casper died in 1998. Eric Thompson had a stroke—he used to come to Central for all his speech therapy—and he died in his early 50s. Eric and Phyllida Law's daughters are Sophie and

Emma Thompson. James Maxwell became an Artistic Director at the Royal Exchange, and he died in his late 50s. Michael Elliott died in his early 50s from kidney disease. Michael and Rosalind Knight's daughter, Marianne, directs a lot at the National and got the Evening Standard award for her *Much Ado About Nothing*.

Lolly: Your connection to the Royal Exchange remained very strong because of that group.

"I worked with George to create the play within the play for the Theatre 69 production of **Hamlet** at the 1968 Edinburgh Festival. Exceptionally for that time—when directors were autocratic and indeed could be dictatorial—George invited us to share in the creation rather than merely be part of the staging. His generosity and vision, his ability to hold the creative process together and at the same time give us the chance to contribute was remarkable and something for which, as a young performer, I felt deeply grateful."

Malcolm Rennie, Actor

George: Yes, there was always a huge connection between Central and the Royal Exchange, and right through into the '70s I did a lot of music for them. I've been lucky to work with good people. At the Royal Exchange, they were the very best.

Lolly: So the Royal Exchange grew out of Theatre 69, which referred back to the 59 Theatre Company at the Lyric, Hammersmith in 1959?

George: Illogically, Theatre 69 really started with *Hamlet* in '68 at the Edinburgh Festival with Tom Courtney as Hamlet. Litz did the movement and I did the music—there wasn't much—and we directed the Players dumb show for the king. We worked for weeks at a separate rehearsal studio, and given that it only lasted three minutes it was scarcely a surprise that it was the most polished part of the evening.

Lolly: Why did they start Theatre 69 in Manchester and not London?

George: Michael and Casper wanted a permanent company and they thought that London was too fashion conscious—you

"George Hall was the most wonderful teacher. It should also be said that he was (probably still is) as good as the best actor in telling a story or the best comedian in delivering of a joke. I don't know whether his perfect timing had something to do with him being a brilliant musician, but listening to him speak was always informative, engaging and often blisteringly funny. At the memorial service for Litz Pisk, George telling a packed church about his long friendship and working relationship with her was not only warm and loving it had everyone laughing out loud. He is a total star. When, as young students, we were lost at sea in rehearsal and scared stiff we would fail and be laughed at by not only the audience but strangers in the street, and probably for the rest of our lives, George had an uncanny knack of imbuing us with the courage of HIS convictions. It was a mystery how he did it but if George said it would be fine, it would be. Encouraging his students to be better than they thought they could be was one of George's many gifts. I will always be grateful to him for that."

Geoffrey Case, Writer

would get a public that would desert you two seasons later—and they wanted to create an audience that would come to everything. It was a deliberate decision to go again to Manchester—what I called the 'Manchester Tendency'. We kept going back.

They were a success from their very first season. Most of the 69 Company's shows that first year were sold out. Vanessa Redgrave worked for them; Eric Thompson, James Maxwell and Braham Murray became leading directors. But their residency at the University Theatre was always tenuous and they were looking for somewhere more permanent, so in the '70s the notion came about to use this odd building in the centre of Manchester, the old Corn Exchange.

To start, they built a tent in the main entrance hall, then they built the theatre. That theatre was always unlike any other. Two things were especially wonderful about it. First, the building already existed, so you didn't need the kind of architect who knew everything about how you did plumbing and toilets; Richard Negri was able to function as a 'sort of' architect, with a marvellous architect working with him. That meant you had a designer's theatre. Richard's image for it was a rose and if you think about it, that's exactly what it was. I once did a lecture about the Vic School connection to the Royal Exchange for the Society for Theatre Research. The architect who did the theatre came up to me and said, 'A building can only be as good as the architect's briefing. Richard knew exactly what he wanted, so it was a triumphant design.'

In 1966, we started to get the second-years at Central to do scenes from plays that were designed by Richard's students at Wimbledon School of Art as part of their diploma exam. That went on for a few years and there were some extraordinary pieces. They were all done in the round and I really think Richard used a lot of what he found out through those exercises—regarding the relationship between the audience and the actors—for his design for the Royal Exchange in Manchester.

The other great strength was that they sat down with everyone who would work in the theatre and asked them questions. They asked the actors things like, 'Would you rather have a small room on your own or a large dressing room with three or four people? Would you like a day bed? Would you like access to a bath or a shower? What do you feel about canteen facilities?' So it was the most actor-friendly theatre imaginable and therefore actors liked to work there. They asked the wardrobe people about how far they should be from the stage, where should the quick change room be and where should they have the wig department. They planned for a canteen that ran from breakfast until the end of the show.

We all had these extraordinary weekends where we did mock-ups. Richard wanted to build a theatre in the round and keep everyone in the audience close to the stage and that meant having fairly steep tiers of seats. I remember one Sunday perched on the top of a frightfully scary ladder, with Richard saying, 'Now, if you were seated up there, what would you see?' Then he went away and designed this wonderful theatre.

Lolly: This was all happening while you were at Central?

"I certainly remember all the fun stories about George...his saying in reference to the Stage '81 late night show, 'I woke up this morning and said to John, "I can't find my opening!"' Now, some of these stories may have actually happened but in the retelling over the years they have become gospel truths. Every year since I left Central, we connect over drinks and dinner in NYC. His advice and wisdom continue to have an impact on my life and my career. He once said to me, "When you have a thousand things to accomplish, you take them down from the shelf one at a time and you get them done...one at a time. And then miraculously, they all get done. Try to do everything at once and you are lost." This bit of wisdom has helped me through twenty years in television production...writing, producing, directing and eventually managing a large and quirky staff. In fact, there are dozens of people who have worked with me over the years at various television channels who have benefited from George's wisdom and don't even know it. The other big 'George lesson', one that has helped me immensely in the crazy world of television, was something he said while directing a second-year production: "The essential ingredient of any successful production is to make sure that everyone involved... from the director to the designers to the actors...*everyone* needs to be telling the same story." This simple piece of advice has been the single most important lesson that I ever learned in terms of getting a group of creative people to work together on any project."

Peter Risafi, Writer, Producer, Director

George: Yes, and when work came up, it often meant fitting in an hour here or there at the school. Sometimes it was writing music; sometimes it was working with actors. Work was not always with the Exchange, but it was often with those same people. I did some vocal coaching for *Good Companions*, which was based on the J. B. Priestley novel and starred Judi Dench and John Mills. Braham Murray directed it, Ronnie Harwood wrote the book, Andre Previn wrote the music and Johnny Mercer wrote the lyrics. Christopher Gable, who had been a star dancer with the Royal Ballet, needed work on his voice and he became a great friend. When he founded the Central School of Ballet, I taught there and became a Governor. And there was a girl who was to play Susie Dean, who had no musical experience and needed help. At the time, I was overwhelmed with work at Central so I had no choice but to say, 'I can see you for an hour on Thursday between this time and that,' so Johnny Mercer and Andre Previn would come to the school every few days. In retrospect it seems like I was being a diva, but I was so busy that I really had no choice. The show came into Her Majesty's and had a moderate run. I was sometimes in rehearsals and it told me so much about Judi Dench's talent. Every time anything changed, when they threw out songs or rewrote scenes, she would say, 'Braham, tell us the story.' I think 'the story' is very central to Judi's talent. Frank Hauser said that when he wanted her to do *The Promise,* she didn't read the play—he went to supper and told her the story.

I worked with Braham again on the *Black Mikado* at the Cambridge, which was *The Mikado* with an entirely black cast except for Michael Dennison as the Lord High Executioner. I was to be the vocal coach, but in fact there was no vocal coaching needed—I just had to become unpopular with the band. The parts weren't written down and they were jazz musicians, so they'd embroidered and embroidered and I had to say, 'The reason she's not audible isn't because she's not audible it's because the trumpet's playing over her.' The band keenly resented it. There was this amazing gospel singer and she sent a message saying, 'Could you come to my dressing room?' She'd taken everything off except for a tiny pair of knickers—and she was enormous—and she said, 'Now listen, I want to ask you. Where in this town can I get good orchestration?'

Lolly: Didn't you also work on the film, *Isadora?*

George: Litz did the choreography and I was an 'unofficial' musical assistant. There was a very good musical director, Anthony Bowles, who wrote the score, but Litz and I chose specific pieces for the film from the music that Isadora Duncan had originally used in her dances. The director, Karel Riesz, was going to use a very big soundstage and we needed a space larger than any rehearsal room, so we worked in a huge London Transport garage in Hampstead with double-decker buses all around. Litz and I did sessions there with Vanessa Redgrave, and there was a lot of 'running about' choreography. Oddly, Isadora had a very uncharacteristic first job in a cheesy chorus line in the follies and, as Litz didn't know any cheap dance steps and I knew nothing but, together we put together this vaudeville routine. One of the joys of that job was getting to know Karel Riesz and his wife, the actress Betsy Blair.

Lolly: By that time, you and Litz were both at Central. How did you end up there?

George: John Blatchley, who'd been on the staff at the Vic, had been running the acting course at Central. In the summer term of '63, there was a falling out between the movement teacher, Yat Malmgren, and the Principal, Gwynneth Thurburn. Blatchley said 'If he goes, I go,' and he did. The first- and second-year students still had three weeks to go, but they couldn't do any of their shows because half the people in their plays had followed Blatchley and Yat to start up Drama Centre. Litz and I were brought in through Virginia Snyders—Ginny had been at the Vic, too, so again it was that connection. She phoned to see if we could devise some work for the remaining students and I did a short course on musical theatre. At the end of the three weeks, that was supposed to be the end of it.

Litz had been teaching two or three hours a week of historical dance classes at Central for Blatchley, but by that time she was mostly teaching pottery at Camberwell Art School. When Central asked her to take over the movement, she had to give Camberwell a term's notice, so until she was free, I stood in for her as movement teacher. I stayed and continued to teach musical theatre, and in the spring of '64 they asked if I'd stay on to run the course.

I have to say, a lot of what was in place at Central had come from Ginny Snyders and John Blatchley, so when I arrived it was almost entirely the Vic syllabus. And, of course, the Central voice training was superb. I'd spent years trying to put together in my own head what I thought speech and voice should be and I thought I'd worked out a whole attitude to voice teaching, a whole attitude to breath. I thought I'd come up with a lot of original things—only to get to Central and find they had for many years been the foundation of Gwynneth Thurburn's thinking. She was totally dedicated and extremely idealistic, and her feeling for speech was magical. She really thought people were impoverished if they didn't have a richness of vocabulary and freedom of voice. The marriage of her vision with that of Litz Pisk created an extraordinary force. And I must say, Thurbie's openness about every change I made was extraordinary.

Lolly: What kind of changes did you make?

George: Litz's great advice to me was to not try to change everything at once, but right away I felt that something needed to be done about the third-year shows. They were unbelievably dreary to look at. The first time Litz and I saw one, she went ashen and said, 'One could never bring anyone to see anything here.' Vic shows had been fantastically designed by people who went on to be leading designers for the next forty years: Central had a series of battleship-grey flats, which they shuffled about the stage. And although they had an extensive wardrobe and professional staff, no one was responsible for the overall look of the shows. Up to that point Central had never had anything designed. Can you believe that?

Every year the students toured a play to Averham, and my first year I was asked to direct one. Very grandly I said, 'I can't work without a designer.' But of course there was no money. My fee was a hundred pounds, so I paid fifty pounds to Clare Jeffery to design. Thurbie was knocked over by the result. The next year, I got them to employ Clare and she came and made it all very professional—and with great tact, I might add. A few years later, we did a show at the Exchange and Clare used David Lewis as an assistant, so we got him to come to Central, too. David was much less inhibited by tact, so the design shot up again. He just wouldn't take no for an answer. Opposed by dreadfully negative attitudes that implied 'No! You can't do that!', in the middle of the night he would break into the scene shop with students to paint the flats and the scenery. The set would arrive the next morning and be terrific.

It was very odd when I first got to Central. They used to lock the building up at 6 o'clock and it was turmoil to them to think we had to use the theatre more. All through my time there I was criticised by governors and people from the world of education who'd say, 'Why do you work the students so hard?' It always amused me that they'd often in the next breath say, 'I did enjoy the last play. We saw it in the West End and we enjoyed it more here.' The connection between long rehearsal hours and a good result seemed to escape them.

And the whole presentation of third-year shows was so dull. They gave two evenings and one matinee, there was no bar, the programme was a bit of typewritten paper. Stage management students started producing delightful programmes. We got the bar going. We started doing four, then five performances.

Lolly: By the early '60s, Central had started to do more shows every year, but prior to that leaving students at all drama schools only did one public show a year, right?

George: Called a Matinee. They'd take a West End theatre and do scenes where students would only have about eighteen lines each; but that was in the time when there was a huge repertory theatre circuit and it didn't matter all that much because we all walked into jobs. You didn't have an employment crisis until you'd been in rep three or four years and thought you might want to start saying 'no' to work—except to go into town or to a better job. It wasn't like if you didn't get performance experience in training you would never get it. Future performance experience could be taken for granted, and the third-year of training was always curtailed so that students could go into the many rep companies that operated in the summer.

When I arrived, 'public' shows in the Embassy Theatre were for family, friends and people in the business. We changed that early on and it was so much fun! I'd done a production in December '65 of *The Italian Straw Hat* by Eugene Labiche and Marc-Michel that had Stephen Bradley, Joanna Moore-Smith, Wendy Allnutt, Sue Lefton and Will Knightley—Keira's father—and we decided to give it a week's run in January '66. We hired a barrel organ and gave balloons to children—to make a splash on the corner of Eton Avenue and to say: 'This is your theatre.' For the first time we made audiences pay for tickets. We made the third-year as close as possible to a season in professional theatre. We did fourteen or fifteen productions and, a few years after I got there, we started doing a late night cabaret show. The place started to have a theatrical buzz.

"George was never cool—the Donovan cap and perpetually raised eyebrow saw to that—but he was sharp, engaged, canny and compassionate. He had a natural, unforced authority and was always patient and encouraging, but he wasn't averse to forcefully reminding the lazy and the unprepared that they were entering a precarious profession in which success was not guaranteed or even probable. We sometimes questioned elements of the teaching regime—it was the '60s after all—but we knew George always had our best interests at heart. When I left Central, I wanted him to think well of me. Actually, I still do."

David Robb, Actor

Lolly: So, in 1963 the course syllabus was very similar to that of the Vic School, but did you develop your own philosophy for training actors?

George: I'd had very strong notions about training ever since the Vic and a lot of what I thought was a reaction to the sternness and the severity of that training. I used the ideas and a lot of the idealism, but what I think I brought was a major alteration to the Vic 'atmosphere'. That was conscious. You go to a showing, it's either a triumph or a disaster, now let's do the next one. It wasn't a matter of suicide if you had a disaster in one play, because you might be great in the next one. That simply becomes the atmosphere and it matters a lot. A lot.

The other very important thing was a refusal to have a 'method'. Different actors work in different ways and each one must be respected. There is no particular morality about ways of working. I think Stanislavski left us slightly burdened with the feeling—it's not what he says, but it's from the tenor of his writings—that there is something less worthy about working from the outside in than there is working from the inside out. Now nearly everybody feels that it's slightly wicked—like secret drinking—to work from the outside in, and yet I think most good actors do both. It isn't a matter of moralizing; it's a matter of respecting whatever produces an exciting result.

Lolly: And those two things—atmosphere and absence of method—changed the training that was in place?

George: The first year I was there, a lot of the structure stayed the same, but it gradually changed and was always changing, and that came about through a lot of discussion with the staff. We endlessly talked about what we should be doing. The biggest difference I made early on was the personnel. There was something in the staff collectively that was fairly buoyant—if not 'jolly' people, they were very positive and philosophical about disasters.

One of the first people I brought in was David Terence, who I hardly knew. He had been very young when he was a student at the Vic—he was in the same year as Avril Elgar and Dilys Hamlett—and we had been in rep together. My instinct was that he'd be a good teacher and director. I never knew anybody who was as capable of putting his finger on what was wrong with a show as David. He was so penetrating. Anything I said, he could see what was wrong with it. He could see the flaw in everything and it was marvellous. There's a non-conformist streak in him that is anti-cosy and so very valuable, even if you don't always like it at the time.

I brought in Bill Hobbs to teach fencing and B. H. Barry to teach stage fighting—both were the very best in almost a completely new field. When I got to Central, they didn't have stage fighting, they had fencing: 'You've been to Nottingham once too often, Master Hood,' and lunge. And I brought in a lot of theatre people who were out there in the real world. It broadened the approach, offered different ways of working and kept us all from relaxing into a private vocabulary. Bruce Robinson, the guy who wrote *Withnail and I*, once told me a wonderful story. He was going through a very bad time in the training and Eric Thompson came in and said, 'Why are you slouching like that?' and Bruce said, 'I've got this shoulder tension.' Eric said, 'Well, why can't you develop a bit of back tension and sit the fuck up?'

Ann Morrish was an actress who had been at the Vic, and she was just overflowing with abundant life. Braham Murray and Michael Elliott came and directed. In fact, that's really where Michael created his production of *Family Reunion*: he did it later at the Exchange and brought it to the Roundhouse, but he did it first

"All I can think about George Hall is charm. A sweetness in life."

Bruce Robinson, Writer

"My memory from my time as a student was of a man of unstoppable energy, beautiful legs and charming tap shoes. He used to take the Stage Management students—of which I was one—for 'movement'. This alone speaks of an inspired, brave and unusually visionary teacher! I've no idea if this idea was his or it was forced upon him, but to even try and take stage management through the basics of actor movement classes reveals a man of huge patience and courage. A man with a vision for training and a passion for co-theatre workers to share a real knowledge of what the whole team does. He also taught us musical theatre where his knowledge and understanding was simply extraordinary. On a personal note, I am hugely grateful to him for having seen the seeds of directorial possibility in me long before anyone else did. He gave me confidence and employment in the years immediately after I left Central. Later I realised that he was watching even when one felt unobserved, and that he had a fantastic talent for reading potentials and futures. Or perhaps he was just impressed by my legs…"

Deborah Warner, CBE,
Director—Theatre, opera and film

"My posture, or rather lack of it, was a cause for some concern the day I auditioned for Central—some even suggested it was bad enough to deny me a place altogether—but George felt otherwise: 'Oh I don't know, there must be *something* we can do.' We talk about my posture even now, thirty years on, and he still thinks something might be done about it. That's what I love about George, his optimism. When my wife ran off with the PT teacher and left me without funds, I thought that was it. I rang George to say I wouldn't be returning to Central after the Christmas break. He thought about it for a moment...if there weren't any fees to worry about, could I at least feed myself? I could try. 'Splendid, we'll see you back at school then.' Whilst rehearsing **The Tempest** in Southampton, I remember calling George from a phone box at two o'clock in the morning and sobbing down the line: 'I can't do it George, I can't do it without a proper tune!' He tried to calm me: 'Darling, if there's no tune, you can sing whatever you like and no-one will be any the wiser. Failing that, you drive up here at the weekend with your little tape recorder and I'll write a tune for you.' He didn't have to, it was enough just knowing that he would."

Peter Guinness, Actor, writer

at Central with David Horovitch in the lead. James Maxwell and Ronald Harwood came and taught—and it's where they did their first directing. Ronnie always says to Sara Kestelman when he sees her, 'I taught you everything you know.'

We also had a good record for hiring female directors—earlier than anybody else, I'd like to think—and that continued throughout my time there. Deborah Warner worked for us early in her career—I was terribly impressed with Deborah and I'm very fond of her.

Lolly: Before we talk more about the training, tell me about auditions. Central used to accept far more people than they ever intended to keep, and as the training progressed they'd ask some to leave. They might start with forty-five and end up with twenty or fewer by the third year. How do you feel about that?

George: It's immoral. It was an easy way of auditioning, you see, but it was not very thorough. People then were only auditioned once. In my first few years, we asked to see all the doubtful people again and so the recall day started. Finally, nobody was ever accepted straight off. They'd do a recall with the entire staff and do some classes, to make sure it wasn't a fluke.

There was a hideous amount of staff time that was taken up with auditions, but there was always somebody from the main staff seeing students. The ability to see potential rather than actuality is terribly skilled, or it at least demands a great deal of experience: 'I cannot hear a word of what this girl is saying and her knees are a disaster and her final consonants aren't there, but....' We used to say that after 1500 applicants we wouldn't see anymore. I suppose it's getting worse. There are more actors, more schools.

Lolly: Everybody who wants to get into drama school asks the question: 'What are they looking for?' It's so subjective, isn't it?

George: But our choices were continually being monitored by the response of audiences coming to see the third-year shows and the work students did after they left; and we had a very good track record. The decision of who would be selected was made by the entire staff, not just the directors: Jane Cowell and Bardy Thomas—who knew voices—and Litz or Barbara Caister—the same for movement. But sometimes it was as simple as, 'This year we've got six Hamlet-ish boys and we need a Falstaff. We can't accept another pale and sensitive boy.' A bit of it is that you're forming a company. If they're all terribly, terribly sensitive they'll disappear up their own arseholes. At least some of them had better be jolly. Equally, you could think, 'This is a very jolly year; we need a balance.'

Lolly: That's a consideration at recalls, but at the first audition sometimes it's just a moment of something interesting—just one second of belief.

George: And it can all be a mirage. You can accept someone and then months later say, 'I think she sent her twin sister because we've never seen the talent again.' It's very odd, you see, because I'm not a good auditioner for exactly the same reason that I think I'm a good teacher. I can always see a little something in everyone. If we hadn't had audition panels with David Terence and John Jones, I shudder to think the actors I'd have taken. Nothing has ever frightened me so much as the occasions when I had to do auditions on my own. When it was all based on my opinion alone, I always feared the rest of the staff would say, 'What on earth were you thinking?'

Lolly: Did you immediately change anything in the curriculum?

George: When I arrived, although they did two plays in the first term, they were just 'sitting down'. Nobody was allowed to get up and move. There was a sort of mystique about a 'placing exercise' when you finally were blocked to move, as though they were saying, 'You can do it sitting down, but can you do it standing up and moving?' I changed it to one play a term in the first year, and people were up on their feet immediately.

A lot of drama schools don't do that now. There's a feeling that you must 'find out who you are'—which is a phrase I don't understand because I'm not sure I've found out who I am even now—and that it is somehow a little rude to do a play too soon. I always thought we should get them involved in a play as soon as they arrived. But I now work in a very minor capacity at Guildhall where they don't do a play for ages and ages and I'm deeply impressed by the work those students do later in their training, so the Guildhall are clearly doing something that works very well. I suppose if you have a staff that is passionate, talented and well-intentioned, perhaps it doesn't matter too much how you set up the training?

Lolly: I remember we had Saturday morning play readings that were run by working actors, but really, the timetable wasn't very demanding in the first year.

George: It got much busier in the second year, but first-year students were never overworked. I felt they needed to get used to London: it was very often the first time they'd been away from home. I started the playreadings because I'd suffered from History of Drama at the Vic—'the plays of Goldsmith led to the plays of so-and-so'—and I thought it was much more to the point that actors came in with plays that excited them and that they shared that enthusiasm with the students. I was more interested that the people doing them could talk about the play more than the historical continuity. Those students who were interested would find the continuity for themselves.

Lolly: What kind of plays did first-years do?

George: The first term play was always Modern Naturalism— Modern, in that, say, it could be *Juno and the Paycock*, it needn't be hot off the press. Resident staff directed those shows, mostly because we felt it was important to emphasize the process not the product and staff members understood that limitation very well. These were shown at the end of term to the staff and the cast of the other play—in a room with no scenery and very little costume and props.

In the second term we always did a Chekhov. Each actor was given a different topic for research and they reported back to the group on the music, the politics, the social life in Russia— whatever the production demanded. In the third term, we did one of the lighter Shakespeare plays, which was always in the theatre and finally seen by the entire school. So gradually through that first year students moved from naturalistic—and not too far from their own experience—to Shakespeare, which confronted them with reconciling reality with heightened and poetic language.

In the second year we did two plays a term and brought in more visiting directors. That was valuable in so many ways. If a student had not had too many successes up to that point, an outsider who knew nothing of past failures could provide a new prospective.

"One student in my year had, much to everyone's surprise, given a rather fine end-of-term performance as the Nurse in *Romeo and Juliet*. A very pretty girl, she had padded-up and hurled herself into the role, proving she had all the makings of a good, if somewhat unexpected, character actress. However throughout the term as we beavered away not only at Shakespeare's play but also at the learning of a myriad other skills, this young woman had been, every weekend, pursuing a high-maintenance social life 'commuting' between St Tropez and London where she was having a romance with a night-club owner (needless to say she was the wealthiest member of the year, as I don't think any grant would have covered her air-fares!) At the end of term, we all gathered for the obligatory session of 'crits'—the teachers' review of each student's work and progress. Nerve-wracking occasions, George always handled these with enormous warmth, wisdom and humour which often cloaked painful and necessary truths. Thus it was when he got to his evaluation of Juliet's Nurse. He smiled at the young woman concerned and in his beautiful gentle honey voice said, 'I think you have a decision to make. Do you want to be an actress—or do you want to act?' In a business seemingly nowadays more seduced by 'celebrity' than any real skill and talent, George's question, as with all his teaching, remains as fresh and pertinent today as it did then."

Susan Wooldridge, Actress, writer

They started with a 20th century American play and moved on to a classic comedy—something from the 17th or 18th century—a play that used a more elaborate and formal language, asides, prologues, epilogues and soliloquies. Second term plays were an Ibsen—which demanded reality and imagination—and then something like a Shaw or a Coward that required a mastery of language and an ease of playing. At the beginning of the third term, plays were chosen depending on what the staff felt that particular year might benefit from the most. It could be a Brecht or an Ayckbourn or even a devised piece. The final play was always another Shakespeare. This was shown in the theatre and still not a public performance, but it had far more production values: lighting, sound, costumes, a full stage management team.

Of course, we devoted a lot of time to voice and movement. The first- and second-year groups were split into halves and they got four hours of voice and four hours of movement per week. Every day started with a 45-minute basic voice class and a 45-minute basic movement class, but there were additional classes, as well as private tutorials. Third-years' class time was cut down, but there were more private tutorials and more singing. Voice and movement classes fed into each other and both were about making the voice and the body free—and as responsive and versatile as possible.

In voice it was about eliminating tension, gaining strength and resonance, relating the breath to sound, increasing colour and range—and relating all that to the impulse to speak. And we worked on speech—articulation and tone—but we never asked an actor to adopt Received Pronunciation in his daily life. Learning RP was only about acquiring another, very useful, dialect. In movement, again it was about relaxation, strength and flexibility, but it was also about posture, rhythm, physical imagination and an awareness of space.

In the first year there were also classes in text, verse, music, scenes and monologues. In the second year we added fencing, tumbling, acrobatics and stage fighting, dialects, period dance, musical theatre and make-up. From the mid-'70s, we added tap and jazz classes, as well. It got very busy, but then a series of conflicting demands stimulates growth. That's the fascination of the training process. You go to a movement class where you strain every muscle to get your leg higher and then you go to an acting class where it doesn't matter whether it goes higher or not. Ultimately getting your leg higher may come as the result of not worrying about it. If you're lucky, you arrive at a point where all demands are only one demand: acting the part.

"To say George had a light touch as a teacher would be true but misleading, for he was no lightweight. In the forty odd years since leaving Central I have worked with many more 'heavyweights' than George, but nothing they have said has left such a lasting impression on me as his deceptively simple sayings: 'An actor has to be in two worlds at once...the world of the play and the world of the audience,' or his profound belief that, 'The theatre can be many things, but the one thing it must never be is boring.' He was fond of saying, 'In acting there are no marks for effort.' You have only to substitute the word 'teaching' for 'acting' in that sentence to have some idea of George's seemingly effortless methods."

David Horovitch, Actor

All of the training was so interlinked at Central. I have to tell you about this…in 1964-5, Litz and I did a project called *Movement and Sound*. We thought all the voice teaching was very good, but it was very static and we wanted to look at what happens if you make those sounds while rushing about. We worked on this project with the second-years for an entire year and we did a fifty-minute show in May. It was very successful, so a year later we did it for the BBC as *Explorations*, with Litz and Vanessa Redgrave introducing. It was everybody's first job at the end of their third year. Ask David Horovitch, Wendy Allnutt, Sue Lefton, any of those people—it was an extraordinary experience. They are marked for life. It was awful and I used to dread the sessions—but it was fascinating. It had a lot of singing, a lot of screaming, a lot of extraordinary movement; and somehow it changed the voice teaching. But we never wanted to do it again.

Lolly: You've talked of classes in just about everything except acting.

George: In the first term, we did what we called 'Acting Study'. At the Vic it was called Improvisation—improvisation in that it was 'made up', imagined by the actor and not based on written text, but not what we have now come to think of as improvisation, with witty actors performing sketches made up out of the air. At the Vic, students were asked to recreate events from their daily lives using imagined objects—and it focused on non-verbal work. Acting Study came out of those classes, but that name didn't really describe what we were doing. I was keen on the idea that, as well as holding attention through your belief, you were also gradually shaping the experience. I always compared it to thinking that if you told a funny story about what had happened to you on the way to school, by the time you'd told it to two or three people—if you had an instinct for that sort of thing—you'd have shaped it. You learned how much background you had to include to make the point and how much background was too much and bored people. If you are a skilled raconteur, by the time you've told a story two or three times you know how much you need to set it up or even how much is too little. As well as enormous observation and a feeling of physicality, the class exercises were about shaping something to present to people. You find out very fundamental things about shape and rhythm.

Lolly: Why do you think those Acting Study exercises are so valuable?

George: With just the simple act of making a cup of tea—or any other everyday activity in what we called 'private solitude'— you call on imagination, memory and observation. But you can also determine whether you're an actor who apologises and retreats or one who demonstrates and over explains. Or maybe you are unable to resist the inclination to push the audience for a response. Or you might reveal your tendency to over-articulate and over-entertain. Or maybe you sharpen for comic effect or you indulge and make it too long and boring— unaware of the fact that seven minutes of very truly threading a needle is enough to drive people to insanity.

Lolly: There were also classes in Animal Study, in the tradition of Copeau and Saint-Denis. How does that help someone become a better actor?

George: There's observation and some physical skill, obviously, but it bridges the gap between physical imitation and imaginative belief. We sent students to the zoo every week for an entire term and they had to come back and 'act' a different animal every week. Any exact copy of a lion or a lemur is impossible, so actors have to suspend their own disbelief if they are to convince an audience of the transformation. It demands a strong imaginative process—totally relevant to the entire

"On my first day as a student, George gave the class a lecture on the Central course's ideals: 'We're not in the habit of breaking people down and building them back up. If you took apart a clock it's highly unlikely you'd be able to put it back together again. You might get it to tick but it will never chime.' Throughout my training, George remained true to that belief, using only his ability to inspire and nurture with his wit and passion."

Harriet Thorpe, Actress

acting experience. We want to see actors who rise above their limitations, don't we?

I also did mask workshops, which were fascinating and produced extraordinary results. They gave students a feeling of total immersion in the experience that we hoped they could bring into their other work. We did half masks, so there was still voice involved, and full masks, which confined the acting to only the body. Masks gave students a freedom to transform that could be liberating. There was no censoring and it became completely unselfconscious. I shall never forget Colin Hurley trying to set fire to the wastebasket, and I remember keenly resenting the moment when the mask led Saylor Cresswell into eating my sandwich. That kind of thing happened to people all the time.

But really, all the classes were about 'disentangling'— experiencing one thing at a time and without the constraints of text. If I ask you to juggle while riding a unicycle, you don't try to learn both of those skills at the same time. You address them separately and then put them together. So at the same time as they did physical work, in other classes students would work on text.

We started with non-dramatic text, where you are only concerned with enlivening a written text—not concerned with being a character or moving beautifully or doing a dialect. Text in which you are not required to be a character, or in which events are not highly dramatic, points out whether you are vocally dreary or alive. Can you keep us interested without the dramatic content? Text classes moved into different periods that varied in rhythm or pace or structure. How did that affect delivery? We also did verse, which offered a compressed form of writing. A particular word was chosen for a particular reason. Why? And what does the structure tell us?

Lolly: Every student received continual criticism in all those classes—from fellow students and from staff. Is that constant criticism what people mean when they talk about drama schools 'breaking an actor down'?

George: That is a phrase I hate. You only have to tell people to what degree they are failing or succeeding—you only have to create a mirror—and they choose their own moment to 'break down'. Some people have a fairly good progression from being not very good to being better to being much better; other people have to, like drug addicts, go to the bottom. That mustn't be a decision for the staff; it's a decision a student's own nature makes for them. They might resist and resist, but we were forever giving feedback, holding up a mirror: 'It was shaped, but it wasn't authentic,' 'I believed you, but it was boring,' or 'This is what I'm seeing.' In their own time, they have to dissolve the elements of resistance that are stopping their progress. Finding time after time that we were not impressed, that we were still not accepting it as an audience—that's when a student might have a black moment where they think they can't do it at all. And that's the start of them getting it—on a good day.

"The day I met George was the beginning of the rest of my life. Although brought up in the theatre, I had no reason to believe that I had any real talent and was experiencing a terrible adolescent lack of self-esteem. I arrived at my Central audition defeated by a failure to get through the one for the RADA and convinced that a similar failure would mean the end of any aspirations I may have harboured. George greeted me like a long lost friend, with his wonderful twinkling smile, and my terror turned to excitement. I found a well-worn patch on the floor, did my speeches and by the time I left the building I had been accepted for the course. Suddenly a future seemed to beckon. George's generous spirit and *joie de vivre* contributed hugely to developing my confidence and self worth. He has the great gift of seeing the good in people and has an infectious enthusiasm. Here I am, all these years later, still at it in some shape or form, and I will be grateful to him, for all of it, forever".

Belinda Lang, Actress

I've always thought that *Twelfth Night* is a marvellous image of actor training. Many of the characters in the play have a false personality. They are led into a state of chaos and only then do they find their true selves. Litz used to say, 'You have to welcome physical chaos before you find real harmony.'

Lolly: Do you allow actors' tensions to relax because of the work they're doing in classes or can you actually go up and say, 'You're tense right there,' so that they can feel it and address it?

George: You can certainly do that. But equally you can point out their tension and they can go to classes and hear it over and over, but they may still find that they can't perform without that tension—what they've come to believe is 'performing'. Often tension in the body of a performer elicits a misleading response in an audience: 'That was a very emotional and intense performance. I was very involved.' But then you'd be very involved if somebody took an axe to a grand piano, wouldn't you? You'd have a strong reaction, but it wouldn't be an aesthetic reaction. I'm digressing here, but I don't think anybody ever talked about 'energy' until twenty or thirty years ago. Energy was taken for granted. Now I hear people say, 'She has a beautiful energy,' and I don't know what that means. 'Life', yes. 'Vitality', yes. But not 'energy'. It's like saying, 'I had a wonderful car ride because I had beautiful petrol.' Energy isn't a virtue. You can't make the journey without the petrol. And 'energy' is sometimes just misplaced tension. So sometimes your job as a teacher is to be a brick wall—refusing to be impressed by all that tension. 'You make yourself hoarse, the beads of sweat are rising on you, your fellow students are impressed. But I'm not impressed.' And it will only change when *they* stop it.

But then, it's all very mysterious: and sometimes it works the other way around. If an actor has a great success in a show, his spine might become released without anyone going near it. It was a very common thing that, say, eighteen months into Central, somebody had done all the work and still nothing was happening—the voice was still tense and their shoulders were still up to their ears. But the right part in the right play with the right director—and getting laughs—suddenly all of the eighteen months work was useful and available. There's nothing like a success to set you free.

Lolly: So you're getting everything ready for the time that the mind finally says, 'Oh, I get it.'

George: It's like the image of an avalanche in some of Ibsen's work. His Norwegian background gave him a great understanding of the nature of an avalanche. Snow on a mountainside may look solid, but while the outer form remains the same often the interior is dissolving. And a sudden sound might cause the disintegration of what had seemed so solid from the outside. So it is with actors. The inner life changes, but the outer life continues through habit. And anything can trigger that avalanche: a moment in class, the right word from a director at just the right time, a success in a play or in a class. One of the joys of training actors is that you are often delighted by the changes that just happen suddenly. You've been doing the slog of the movement classes

"The first thing we learned as students from George was sensuousness and expressiveness of movement. He could articulate and demonstrate so concisely what all those bizarre and tortuous daily exercises were about and how every movement should emanate from your very core. He had a similar gift for teaching music skills. I remember once having to sing a 'counter-point' duet—'Musical Demon' and 'Won't You Play a Simple Melody?' I was paired with Donna Champion, the best singer in our year and unsurpassable at a raunchy jazz number, while I had quite a melodic voice, in an ex-choirboy sort of way. The casting should have been obvious, but I wheedled Donna into letting me do the jazzy part. Well, we sang it O.K., but George was deeply pained. He grilled me—with that utterly bemused expression of his—why on earth had I thought that duet would work best with my singing 'Musical Demon'? He was gentle and careful not to destroy my confidence, but that one lesson taught me several things: recognize and utilize my own and my colleagues' strength and weaknesses, throw focus to colleagues at the appropriate times, and be a much more supportive actor. I have taken those lessons with me through the years and have been forever grateful."

Kevin Whateley, Actor

"'Eyes and teeth'—that's the phrase which evokes George for me. He used it as he sat at the piano exalting us to be truly present. I'd never heard it before and it, like George, seemed very 'Showbiz'—not quite what I was expecting from drama college in the early'70s. Whatever his style, George is a natural teacher. It's his 'eyes and teeth' that I recall instantly when I think of college and he had the best energy—in every sense—of anyone there—teachers or students."

Lindsay Duncan, CBE Actress

and the voice classes and nothing's changed. Then suddenly that actor is totally different.

I think that's why in a three-year course what is important is not to break an actor down, but for him to break himself down. Until the spine or the voice is really released, the simplest things can sometimes not be available to an actor because of constriction. When someone discovers for the first time they can do a lot more with a lot less energy because they have eliminated tension, they begin to see the possibilities elsewhere.

Lolly: When I first started teaching I remember arrogantly thinking, 'I just told them…whatever… and they got it. You'd have thought someone would have told them 'whatever' before their second year!' How rude was I to assume that everybody hadn't been endlessly telling them these things? Drip, drip, drip. It can be Chinese water torture for teachers, having to say the same thing over and over and finding new ways to try to get through!

George: Darling, I used to think by the end of the first week, 'I've told you everything I know about acting. Now I've got to keep saying it for the next three years until you hear it.'

Lolly: Yet you're relentlessly positive when you teach. In your musicality class at the Guildhall you taught the whole hour-long class and the only negative comment I heard was when the group sang a wrong note and you gleefully said, 'Rubbish!' Everyone just laughed.

George: Karen Rabinovitz is a wonderful teacher because she's so positive and encouraging. I would be struggling with a tap step and I'd do it right once and she'd say, 'YES!' Now, I know she didn't start to think I'm Fred Astaire, and I'm sure that most students aren't misled by praise. When they're encouraged it doesn't make them think that they're better than John Gielgud. But they do sense enthusiasm in your voice about a step taken.

Lolly: Many already have a little gremlin on their shoulder saying, 'Not good enough!'

"My strongest memory is the excruciating discomfort of having to get up and perform music hall songs in front of my sneering (I was certain) peers. The task of conveying quaint lyrics, without parody and with unimpeachable gusto, was one which I can't help feeling was very useful in breaking down the last vestiges of teenage 'cool' that were still holding us (well me, certainly) back. And I always remember George's advice about acting—which was always sage and witty. I still (fail to) heed his warning not to assume that the Chinese gentleman sitting opposite me on the Piccadilly line is sitting there thinking about how Chinese he is."

Rufus Sewell, Actor

George: Yes, but then we often have to cope with those students who arrive with Amateur Dramatics false confidence, about which you've actually got to say: 'It's not that.' It's both complicated and very simple.

Lolly: Saint-Denis wrote of a four-year training. Central has done a three-year course for many years. Now there are a lot of one-year post-graduate courses. Do you think there is an optimum length of time for training an actor?

George: Obviously you can't tailor a course for everybody's different specifications. One always knew that three years of training was a very arbitrary thing, that some people might be all right after two and some people might need four or five. There were two experiences after leaving Central that were quite an eye-opener for me: doing individual singing lessons, and teaching at places like the Poor School where students had classes on evenings and weekends for two years. At Central I'd

"As I continue to work with George, I never cease to be amazed by his naïve enthusiasm, wit and love of teaching. I remember during my early days at Central having to spend weeks exploring 'getting up in the morning'. We had to be incredibly detailed in every aspect that this entailed. Then one day he turned it on its head and asked us to encapsulate the work in the form of a 30 second TV commercial. This was extraordinary in its simplicity and profundity, as we had to extract something minute from all the detailed research we had done—I've never forgotten it. As a teacher myself now, I have often used some of George's exercises. Again and again, I have found myself amazed by how multi-layered these apparently facile exercises are. It is an absolute privilege to have him working with our team at the Guildhall School of Music and Drama. Despite his age, his energy is boundless. I do not believe he is any different from the teacher I knew as a teenager. Arriving from Brighton in his peak cap, with a smiling face and music hall songs tucked under his arm, always ready to pass on to the next generation the connection between singing and acting. Anyone who has had these classes will never forget them."

Wendy Allnutt, Actress, Head of Movement at the Guildhall School of Music and Drama

always fit into a tutorial pattern of a less intensive kind and I'd never done individual coaching, so when I saw somebody at least once a week for a couple of months it was a surprise to me how much people could improve. For some, one year can be fearfully rushed, and if you start a course where people are going to leave twelve months later, you have a different attitude to the degree to which you can tell them everything that's wrong with them. You can't leave them unfinished at the end of their eleventh month, but you can leave them pretty unfinished at the end of the first year of a three-year course.

Lolly: You still teach the history of musical theatre to students?

George: Yes, at the Guildhall I always say that I represent the 'common element', but I think that is so important. It's the vitality of the theatre. And really it's all about playing records of extraordinary artists from Broadway musicals, opera and music hall.

Lolly: What is it about music hall that is important for actors?

George: Music hall stars were not particularly good singers, but they had wit and they had acting skills. Character, conviction and the words convey the meaning as much as some abstract beauty of the sound.

I still do music hall at the Guildhall and the RAM, and with fear and trembling I go to this cool generation with these naïve songs. If you are twenty-one, there is no reason you should know that funny or absurd songs exist. There are no songs about daily life in the pop world. There are none about 'I parted my hair in the middle' or about Matilda who'd left her false teeth out and they'd clamped onto somebody. But these young kids just love them. It's so much fun. You, know everything journalists write about the young confounds me, because I am surrounded by enchanting young people—sensitive, well-mannered. Where are all these monsters?

Lolly: And you teach 'musicality'. What is that?

George: I originally went to the Guildhall to do music hall songs.

"As head of the course George exemplified so much that was excellent in the theatre. With an apparent casualness to his work, it gradually became obvious to us that this pose masked a wholly disciplined and yet passionate love of theatre and its practitioners. But his greatest gift was and is his enthusiasm for all forms of theatre and entertainment. Today, theatre seems frequently to be subdivided into exclusive sects that rarely interact with each other, but in the 1960's the theatre was still a populist force. Many regional theatres, like football clubs now, sold at least half their tickets as season tickets before productions opened. Important openings both in the West End and elsewhere were frequently covered on the front page of quality papers and even the most downmarket papers had a fulltime theatre critic. In this environment, George made us look at areas that we, in our youthful arrogance, might otherwise have overlooked. He opened my eyes to the great pleasure of musical performance, giving it as much status as any other type of performance, and under his tutelage I became a much more versatile performer than I had ever thought possible."

Malcolm Rennie, Actor

Somebody else was doing music notation and when they retired I heard myself, to my horror, saying, 'I'd be quite interested to see if I could find a different way of doing that.' I'm still fascinated. An instrumentalist has to know the names of notes; a singer only has to know relationships. 'Do So' isn't an absolute, it's a relationship; and it's fascinating trying to find a way of making that clear.

"George has had an enormous impact on my career and is quite simply one of the world's greatest and most inspirational of teachers. His classes were never less than exhilarating; his weekly seminars were a revelation and covered every aspect of the entertainment industry—from theatre history to sex, drugs and rock 'n roll. He encouraged us to see everything: from Olivier at the National and Fonteyn and Nureyev at the Opera House, to the rock musical *Hair* and Vanessa Redgrave in Antonioni's *Blow-Up*. His approach was holistic— 'Experience everything'—and he suggested that we revel in versatility, that we 'maintain the right degree of cynicism' so that we would not be too distraught about the disappointments. These things—plus a sense of humour: pretty good guidelines. We were chatting a few years ago and I admitted that I was having a tough time with a part in a play. He responded, 'Nobody ever said it was going to be easy.' It isn't, but George's influence has certainly made it more enjoyable."

Nickolas Grace, Actor

Lolly: You could make a point that actors don't need to know how to read music.

George: No, but they need rhythm and they need musicality.

Lolly: In the classes I visited at the Guildhall, you handed out four-part harmonies to the groups and didn't play the music on the piano until they'd put it together and sung it themselves. That was only their fourth class and they were able to do it.

George: They can read the music because it's the relationship in notes they're reading. I did some of that at Central when I taught singing.

Lolly: Did you start directing musicals at Central immediately after you took over?

George: The first I did was *Maria Marten* in '65. The next year I did *Down in the Valley* by Kurt Weill. I did *Giroflé-Girofla*, which is like an Offenbach, but by his rival Lecocq. I often think that is the favourite production I've ever done. Mickey Feast was superb. Deborah Grant was smashing. I had Pat Heatley, who had a lovely voice, and Gloria Connell and a wonderful guy called Neil Kennedy, who died of AIDS much later. Bruce Robinson was in it—he was charming. And David Dundas, who later had a hit record and became a big music producer. It was a stunning cast. They got the feel of the absurdity and the musicality of that 19th century style and I was more proud of it than any production I've ever done. It's a wonderful score and I translated it and rewrote it, because I thought the plot wasn't properly articulated. By the first rehearsal, I hadn't done any of the lyrics so they learnt the whole thing to 'la la la'. Someone swore there were still two lines of 'la-la-la' up until the dress rehearsal.

Then, with Stage '68 I did a musical called *Two Bouquets*, by Herbert and Eleanor Farjeon. It was an Offenbach-type piece using existing Victorian tunes, and the Farjeons wrote new lyrics.

"My first job when I got out of Central was with Theatre 69, playing Hermia in *Midsummer Night's Dream*, for director Braham Murray. After I'd been out of Central a year or two, George asked me to do *Guys and Dolls* for the same company and I said 'George, I can't sing!' 'There's no such thing,' he said. That complete optimism and belief that he projects onto you is rare, and his encouragement to do Adelaide was the best thing that could have happened to me. Doing it led to so many other things, and if I'd never done another musical, doing *Guys and Dolls* would have been enough."

Zoe Wanamaker, CBE, Actress

Lolly: And the 1969 *Guys and Dolls* was the first Broadway musical?

George: I had done four songs from *Guys and Dolls* for an Open Day for Central's 50th Anniversary and again for Thurbie's retirement. They went down very well and that emboldened me to do the whole musical. Nickolas Grace played Nathan Detroit, David Robb was Benny Southstreet, Lynda Bellingham played Sarah, and Lee McCain was Miss Adelaide. Robin Nedwell was the Cuban nightclub dancer. I believe it was the first time that any of the drama schools—as opposed to stage schools—had done a big Broadway musical. The Vic School had believed a great deal in song and dance, but they would no more have done a Broadway musical than die.

I don't think even reps did Broadway musicals until we did *Guys and Dolls* in '72 with Theatre 69 in Manchester. The received wisdom was that if you were going to do one, you had to do an absolute replica with full orchestra. Well, we did it very simply with two pianos and a drum, because that's all we could afford. Zoe Wanamaker was a wonderfully funny Miss Adelaide, and Trevor Peacock was stunning as Nathan. Mickey Feast was an unforgettable Nicely-Nicely and it also had a number of other ex-students from Central, some of them directly from the course and into their first jobs.

Lolly: These days there is a proliferation of musical theatre courses that serve musicals all over the country.

George: When I was at Central we did musical theatre and singing only as part of the acting course, with no separation. We just taught our actors how to sing. Tyrone Guthrie said, 'I can't work with actors who aren't musical.' He was talking about actors having sensitivity to form as well as to content, as well as having a rhythmic vitality.

Lolly: Saint-Denis talks about it as the 'pulsation of the text'. How do you train somebody in rhythm?

George: You have to assume that rhythm is inherent. Your heartbeat is rhythmical. It's universal. So it's not how you teach rhythm, it's how you unblock it. Training an actor is about releasing physical and emotional tensions that disturb a natural process. When you've uncovered those, people are rhythmic.

I often think that rhythm is hugely underrated in the theatre. The difference between actor A and actor B may not be imagination but rhythm. It's a cliché to say that a great sculptor senses the shape in a shapeless bit of stone, but that is really its essence. If you write music for a Shakespeare song you feel the music is already in there. It's not an invention; it's an unlocking. Maureen Quinney, who was at the Vic with me, did a recording with Edith Evans. Edith kept saying, 'If you don't give me the right tune on my cue, I can't do it.' She had worked with William Poel, who started the Elizabethan Stage Society in the 19th century, and Poel felt that all of Shakespeare had a 'tune'. Edith used to say, 'I think Poel liked me because my voice did go up and down.' The tunes and the rhythm were so terrific with Edith Evans.

Lolly: You worked with her for television. Her stage presence was so 'large'. How did she bring that down for the small screen?

George: Stuart Burge directed her in her first ever television. He said: 'I'm sorry there are so many people around in the studio, but they are all there for a purpose,' and Edith said, 'That's quite all right. They all have their jobs to do, and the only other people are the cameras. And they're all friends, aren't they?' Then she smiled into each camera. That is genius.

" I hear George talking about 'this notion' of the breeze flowing through the flute in the tree, an image of relaxed voice production that I still find inspiring and useful. I hear him talking about Sinatra and Billie Holiday and phrasing and breathing and stolen time. He could combine analysis with his love and feel for the music so that you never lost sight of the fact that you were learning to perform—to actually get on your feet and do it yourself. I hear him in the weird little lecture theatre, which was actually the sawn-off walled-up bit of the back of the Embassy balcony, relating his experiences of 'the business'. Someone asks him if it is as much of a rat race as we had heard. George raises the eyebrow, smiles and says: 'It's only a rat race if you turn into a rat and start running.' George taught me everything I needed to know in order to continue learning."

Michael Feast, Actor

Training students to face television cameras has always been tricky because it seems to me that the most difficult thing about working in that medium is the fact that you are in someplace the size of an aircraft hanger with a lot of people you haven't met. You can't train someone for that and you can't simulate those conditions in any way at a drama school. Yet many of our students went on to become very successful in TV and film, as well as in the theatre.

Lolly: Did you have instincts about which students would succeed?

George: They were so often wrong that you stop having them. That's one of the traps of theatrical biographies. People say,

"I channel George all the time in my work as a film director. So many times I have the thought, 'Oh, God, what George could do with this actor in one afternoon!' In 1994, I sent the great Leslie Caron (Gigi, for God's sake) to George to rehearse her song 'Englishmen Don't Make Love By Day' for my film, *Funny Bones*. George sorted her out in a couple of sessions. But I wanted him 'there' on the day of filming that song, so I cast him as the club pianist. I felt safe. We filmed the song 'live', no cheating, no playback. I'm starting rehearsal tomorrow with America's biggest teen star and all I can think is: 'How can I get George Hall into my briefcase!'"

Peter Chelsom, Actor, Director,
Writer, Producer

"I was a baby when I arrived at Central—barely seventeen when I auditioned, barely eighteen when I arrived—and almost everything that was happening to me while I was there was happening to me for the first time. It was where, predictably, I fell in love for the first time and a few months later, also predictably, it was where I first got dumped. When it happened I didn't know what to do and so I simply walked out of classes (another first) and disappeared. Being eighteen I got over the heartbreak in a couple of days but spent a few more AWOL anyway, desperately trying to think of something to say to my tutors when I finally went back. I still didn't know what that something would be when, a week or so later, I found myself sitting opposite George and a couple of administrators in his study, having been summoned there once word

'There was this girl in the corner who somehow caught my eye'—and it turns out to be Margot Fonteyn. That's in every book and it's not true. People think 'perfectly ordinary' at the time and then in retrospect they amend their memory.

Lolly: Elsie Fogerty said that when Peggy Ashcroft and Laurence Olivier were students at Central everyone knew they were special. Do you think that could have been the truth?

George: Well, they were living in a time when people went to Central and RADA as finishing schools. Girls learned to be more graceful and speak better. In Olivier and Peggy's year there were about four men and god knows how many women, mostly non-actresses. Peggy said Olivier wasn't at all good-looking when he was a student: he was quite ill groomed; he had a funny hairline, which he then shaved. He re-invented himself as a good-looking young man. Peggy also told me that what Olivier did as a student wasn't very 'theatrical'. But then, Peggy thought very little of Central when she was there as a student. She was very critical.

Success is funny. Some of the most promising people never get anywhere: some have a terrific run of good luck or a terrific run of bad luck. Or you can have looks that are at variance with your talent. Peter Chelsom was a born character actor—his impersonations are wonderful and I'm told his impersonation of me is devastating—but he was a very good-looking young man with no capacity for playing *jeune premier*, so nobody knew what to do with him. The same thing happened to David Dundas, who should have had an amazing career as an actor. His character performances were wonderful. He played an old man in the early John Osborne play, *Epitaph for George Dillon*, and he did a performance, which you thought, 'From your background and your age, where the hell did you find that?' Then he went into the theatre and people cast him as wet young men. Michael Grandage was a terrific character actor, but he gave it up and now is terribly successful as a director. Graham Norton is a far, far better actor than he gives himself credit for. David Dundas became a big music producer. Peter Chelsom is directing in Hollywood now.

had got round that I'd resurfaced. I was nervous and upset—not least because I felt my whole future might depend on how the next few minutes went. I opened my mouth to say something, as interested as anyone else in the room to know what was going to come out. Before anything could, George (who had clearly been briefed on my romantic circumstances) said: 'Are you ok now? Are you...back?' I said that yes, yes I was, but before I could flesh this out George said, 'Good'. And looked at me. There was quite a long silence, a silence I spent trying to fathom why he was smiling slightly. After a while, he raised his eyebrows in an unspoken 'Well?' and waited for me to get the hint and leave the room. Which, eventually, bursting with relief and gratitude, I did. No punishments, no warnings, no lectures: just an innate understanding that many of the younger students in his care still had some growing up to do and that from time to time Life would get in the way of the curriculum. It was exactly, exactly the right way to handle the situation. Very few would have seen that. On George's watch the tuition at Central was excellent; the pastoral care was second to none."

Neil Pearson   Actor, writer

Lolly: You keep track of a lot of your old students, don't you?

George: It's interesting to see where they go, what they do. I remember when Neil Pearson started Central; he was about seventeen and felt very undereducated. Rob Demeger, who was

"On our final day at Central, George gathered Stage '87 together in Room B at the top of the school. He congratulated us and said we probably thought we had been at the college for the last three years so that we could all become famous actors, however, this had not been his aim. His purpose had been to make us more rounded and fuller people, so that we might be better equipped for whatever we went on to do in life—a vision that was then well beyond our comprehension."

Peter Hamilton-Dyer, Actor

in his year, had been a schoolmaster, so Neil got a reading list from Rob and the entire three years he read a play a day and a novel a week. He is now the most formidably well-read person. He wrote a book recently about English books published in Paris in the '30s by the Olympia Press—the ones who published James Joyce and William Burroughs when nobody else would touch them. Neil had become a collector and started to do a bibliography; it turned into a book.

Lolly: Central students were being educated in ways you couldn't predict and in ways that were not always quantifiable. When Elsie Fogerty started Central in 1906, her desire was to get diplomas for her students, but now most drama schools have to award degrees to get funding. How do you feel about degrees for actor training?

George: In careers like music and ballet there are basic skill requirements: I don't think it's the same for actors. Anything you say an actor must be able to do I can think of amazing actors who can't do them. I think of Wilfred Lawson, who couldn't quite speak Standard English and wasn't always audible and didn't exactly say the text—yet you knew you were watching great acting. That for me is the reality. He wouldn't have got a degree. The history of the theatre is littered with too many of these stories. Alec Guinness did a term somewhere and they said, 'We're going to give you your money back. It's a shame to take it because you'll never, never be an actor.'

I'm endlessly thinking of my teacher, Percy Harris. She was one of the great influences of my life—her sense of what design meant in the theatre and how it should serve the play.

Quite into her old age Percy started the Motley Studio to train designers. She always thought that art schools made a dreadful mistake by going for degree status because she thought that was nonsense in terms of visual arts. She ran the Studio into her 90s and she would never compromise, so she was endlessly with the begging bowl just to keep the place alive. The Arts Council kept saying, 'We will subsidise you, but you must fit into the system.' But she wouldn't. I feel like that. I can quite see that from where and when Fogerty started Central a degree was a high goal. But the divergence between rogues and vagabonds and going up to get a scroll of paper doesn't mesh for me.

Lolly: Is that why you left Central? It was around the same time that the big push for degrees started.

George: No, it was a number of things. The job was becoming more and more about administration and less about teaching and working with students. There was a good pension on offer from the ILEA, of course, but really it was just time.

Lolly: You didn't really retire after you left Central and you've never slowed down. You even acted again.

George: I'd always had an agent—from the '50s until she retired about five years ago. She was so sweet to keep me on; I made absolutely no money for her. I was always doing things for the Royal Exchange and she'd say, 'Five hundred pounds?' and I'd say, 'They can't possibly afford that!' and would persuade her to take less.

Lolly: What kind of parts have you done?

George: Do you remember the film, *Mrs. Brown*? I was the Speaker of the House, which was practically nothing, but for me it was an outing. I got that through the casting director, Michelle Guish, who had been at Central on the teacher course. And I played 'an elder' in a terrible, terrible film about Samson

"George's roguish twinkle, his profound insight into the human condition, his compassion and his love of music, language and the correlation between the two, are his legacy to his students throughout the world. Almost forty years after I left Central, I was asked to become President of the American Academy of Dramatic Arts in Los Angeles. I had segued from my work as an actor to that of an artistic director and was at the helm of a professional theatre in Massachusetts, when this rather surprising offer came to go back to where I started. I remembered George's raised eyebrow, the slight tilt of the head and the voice that with characteristically upward inflection would say 'Hello', and wondered what he would think of such a journey. When I took on my new responsibilities I often thought of my time as a student, covered in confusion and acne but still nurtured under the watchful tutelage of the great George Hall, and I have used him as a role model in the constant interaction with this new breed of young actors."

James Warwick , Former President, American Academy of Dramatic Arts, LA Division

and Delilah, done by Nicolas Roeg. Elizabeth Hurley was in it and I think it might be the worst film I've ever seen. I did a bit in *Scarlet and Black* in '93, playing Father something-or-other. That was with Alice Krige—remember her from Central? It also had Euan MacGregor and Rachel Weisz. That's where I met Malcolm Sinclair and we became great chums. He made me laugh so much. It was the first acting job I'd done for ages so everything I did Malcolm said, 'Ah, I think you may have left it too long....' Euan MacGregor and I had a long shot wandering away from the camera, walking into this cathedral where he was supposed to have put up things for the glory of god, laughing: 'Darling, I just *love* what you've done with this cathedral!'

Lolly: And you continued to train actors.

George: I was asked to teach at the British American Drama Academy and I became a governor. For awhile I worked at the Poor School with John Jones, Bardy Thomas and Barbara Caister. In 1989, I did a fascinating job, doing a musical theatre course with the students at the National Theatre School in Stockholm. Their concentration level was superior to anything I'd ever known—I'm sure none of them had been to a badly run school.

I'd already been to Stockholm with Nina and Frederik, to play a huge cabaret theatre called Berns. Apropos of nothing, Berns had all top liners—Lena Horne, Harry Belafonte, Marlene Dietrich—and it did this eccentric thing: whoever they were and no matter how big a star, their contract said that on Sunday at five they did a children's performance. The children all had a big cream tea with fishy things and a lady with a funny Welsh witch hat came out and sang folk songs. Then these glitteringly sexy acts like Marlene Dietrich had to come out and perform for these bewildered children. It may tell us something about the curious Swedish psyche?

But one had just never met such efficiency. We were to do a version of 'There's a Hole in My Bucket' and I'd forgotten to take the prop, so I said to this lady stage manager, 'We need a bucket.' Very po-faced she said, 'Oh, yes.' And I'm apologetic, 'And it needs to have a hole in it.' She was totally unfazed, 'Oh, yes. Vich size?' And it was there in about three minutes.

Lolly: Have you done more international work these last twenty years?

George: Now and then. Here and there. I was asked to Milan for a conference on Training the European Actor with Adrian Noble, Cis Berry and Jenista MacIntosh. It was being run by Giorgio Strehler of the Teatro Piccolo in Milan, who was the Peter Brook of European theatre. I was there to talk about what effect Copeau had had on the British theatre.

And in '93, I was invited to the Moscow Arts Theatre School. The school suddenly had no funding and needed money, so we all had to watch a class and then bounce onto television saying what a wonderful school it was and how we'd been influenced by it. They'd phoned me and said, 'We are not putting you in a tourist hotel; we are putting you in a hotel where Russians live!' Well, I wish they hadn't. My eye caught the single tap—there was only one, with cold, cold water. It

"When I started the course at the Royal Academy of Music, I was incredibly naïve as to what that would entail. Karen Rabinowitz introduced me to George towards the end of my first (traumatic) year, and what I have so valued about him is his ability to listen and offer advice (if asked) in the most comforting and unobtrusive way. Always right and objective, his sound appraisal of any situation is backed up by years of experience. When I've been floundering, he's been there—as has John—and a word of praise or acknowledgment has meant a lot, while his 'chuckle' and suppressed giggle has kept me going many a time. Never judgmental, if after a project a student hasn't done as well as we had hoped, it's never criticism but always a positive 'What shall we do about...?' It isn't for sentiment's sake that the students call him 'The Master'. His musical theatre history talks are a legend. 'He was there,' so many of them remark. How refreshing, as George gets older, to hear this looked upon as an asset! His anecdotes and stories of performers and performances are always to illustrate a point or to share an exciting and riveting memory. George is always inspiring—and his quiet, outward calm conceals a vigorous brain and a wonderful musician, able to hear everything in one chord—'Shouldn't that really be minor?' He hears things once and then, on to the piano. Can many people, not just at 85 but at anytime, play any show tune of almost any era by ear, transpose, so easily (envy!) and all this at a New Year's Eve party after quite a lot of wine and champagne? I am full of admiration!"

Mary Hammond, Head of Musical Theatre, Royal Academy of Music

was freezing outside and there was a broken pane in the window—I wore more clothes to bed than I did to go out. I managed to get a flight home that stopped in Vienna and the hot shower in my hotel there was the most erotic experience of my life. The thought of what Russia has now become saddens me. I met a wonderful director who had only been kept alive by sheer cynicism and I remember him saying, 'It's so wonderful now. For the first time, I'm able to sit in a dress rehearsal without some government man sitting by my elbow saying, 'You can't do this play.' I should think for him the bad days are back.

Lolly: During that same period, you also taught at the London Centre for Theatre Studies.

George: Yes, but then the Royal Academy of Music came into my life and I really knew that in a way it was a job that I'd be happy to do all my life, so that really had to take precedence. It was the only time I'd written a job letter for about forty years: 'I came to see a performance at the RAM and I was very impressed by the singing and very impressed by some of the acting, but I thought the comedy was absolutely appalling.' In my conceit I'd thought, 'How dare anyone start a musical theatre course without me?' To Mary Hammond's great credit she called me, despite my critical tone.

Lolly: So, is your work with the singers at the RAM about their singing or their acting?

George: Both, but I also feel terribly grateful that I did so much movement training. There are moments when there's a problem with somebody where it's physical, cum vocal, cum psychological. Maybe the thing you say changes it, or it may be the way you change the state of somebody's shoulders so that they hear a different sound in their voice. I often watch performances and long to run onto the stage and adjust their bodies. That is not an acting thing: it's an instrument thing. So sometimes the solution is acting, sometimes the instrument.

I'm fascinated by the moments where it isn't an imaginative solution but a physical one. Singing a high B flat is not natural—not if you are to be able to do it in a controlled way—and no amount of imagination will achieve that, and what you want in a wonderful musical performance is somebody who is totally convincing but also fulfils the other demands of musicality and form. You may have very good vocal equipment up to A flat and a part demands B flat, and it might take you three or four years to get there. Although it may mean that getting there demands an imaginative process, it is also a technical process. In an ideal world you wouldn't study any technical singing until your voice was totally free. As Mary Hammond says, 'Free the voice, yes, and then *train* the voice.' But find total physical freedom first. It's comes down to that question: 'Is technique a cage or a tool?'

Lolly: There is technique to achieve a great belt or a great vibrato—physical knowledge that an actor may not have—but although an actor may not be able to hit that high note they can imagine their way around it so an audience doesn't notice they're not hitting it, right?

George: People say that Judy Garland was endlessly singing, doing the same line ten different ways and making no decisions; then she just came on and it was the way it was. She did a four-week season at the Dominion in the early '50s, and in one of the performances I saw she had terrible laryngitis. She had a brilliant arrangement by Gordon Jenkins of 'Come Rain or Come Shine', which had bongos, and you can't speak your way over bongos. She came on and she just pushed it thru the air. The intensity was electrifying. All you could hear was the lyric and you thought, 'She doesn't need a voice. It's great when she has one, but the thing that is riveting is the intensity of her belief in the lyric.'

Having said all that, I would still retreat from any interpretation that might suggest that all singing problems are acting problems. Nor are they always physical problems. They're both an oversimplification and lead us down the road toward looking for a 'method'. And, as you know, I certainly think methods don't work in the theatre. If there is a moment that doesn't work, it could be that the actor's not imagining it. Or it could be that the feed line was wrong, or that the actor is imagining it but his articulation isn't good, or that the lighting is too dim, or the actor is too far upstage. It could be a thousand things.

It's almost an image of our age, I think, that the moment something doesn't work, there are a lot of people who want to say there's only one solution to that problem. 'The actors are under lit? How dare you! No, it must be that he's not imaging what it's like to be in 1412.' Often in books people write about acting they offer a method that says that there could be only one thing that is wrong and that one solution will correct everything. I think there is joy in being challenged by a moment that isn't working and trying to figure out exactly what's getting in the way. And it may be as simple as, 'You don't need all that theory, darling. Just pronounce the final consonant and you'll be fine.'

Lolly: You still do revues at the RAM. What is it about cabaret, revue, that is valuable for training both singers and actors?

George: It's wonderful to have two minutes that's entirely you—nothing to do with anybody else or any situation. And you have to learn to look an audience in the eye. Sometimes it shows us a side of a student that has never been seen before.

Lolly: I remember Betsy Brantley in a late night show at Central. She was this fresh-faced American cheerleader type, yet when she walked out on stage that night she turned into Grace Kelly.

George: We had been worried about her being inaudible for two years and then when she sang this huge voice came out. Remarkable!

"Auditioning for Central, I remember thinking that George embodied everything "artistic". As an American, I immediately saw an English Bob Fosse, jazz shoes permanently glued to his feet, his body anxious to explode into rhythm at the merest hint of a suggestion, exhaling a delighted "Ahhhhhhhh!" (with fingers outstretched). George was everything I wanted to be—a creature purely motivated by artistic impulse— exotic! But he was, and is, so much more than that, more than that creative spark. George has soul. Every student knew that George cared singularly for him or her in a way that made each and every one of us unique. I don't know that I've ever met anyone since who carries that degree of graciousness and generosity. I have an abiding image of George from when I was a student. In yet another rowdy class on yet another cold and rainy day, George was fed up. Through our relentlessly juvenile behavior, we had tested even George's patience. As he looked each of us in the eye in turn, he quietly said, 'I have given you everything I know how to give. What do you want - my blood?' And I knew then, as I know now, that had he thought it would have helped, he would have opened a vein on the spot."

Betsy Brantley, Actress

Lolly: There is an assuredness from the performers in your RAM shows. How do you instil that?

George: Part of it is that I don't do any material that I can't have total faith in. If I've got the right song for the right person

"For anyone who knows George as an acting teacher it might surprise them to know that he is also one of the finest piano teachers I've had. While I was at the Academy, I worked with him on a number of projects—doing music hall and 1920s/30s repertoire with the musical theatre students. He is obsessive when choosing material for each individual and once that song is found insists on trying any number of keys to find the right one. This is was the first time I'd been asked to transpose at sight and it was a quick learning curve with George—sometimes adjusting the key just before the performance itself. At first I would busk away just transposing the basic chord symbols, but with a few subtly raised eyebrows it quickly became clear that I wouldn't get away with glibly paraphrasing Richard Rodgers' complex inner voicings! While always self-deprecating about his piano playing, he taught me as much about the technical element of playing as any other teacher I have had—his teaching of phrasing, when to lead and when to follow and most frequently when to just lay down a steady beat for the singer—all skills that I hadn't really been encouraged to think about until the Academy course. Recently, we were at a British Voice Association conference at the Royal Academy. George had given a presentation that morning, and as we listened to one of the lectures that followed he turned to me, grinning, and said, 'Isn't it wonderful that I'm being paid to be here and learn all these new things!'"

Nigel Lilley, Musical director

I suppose I feel very confident of getting them somewhere. Also, I've always thought the greatest piece of advice I've ever heard was Noël Coward's words to Elaine Stritch: 'Always work with people who know more than you do.' The joy of being at the RAM is that I'm surrounded by such people. When I did cabaret shows at Central, I played the piano, staged the numbers and very often, god forgive me, fixed the dances. Now at the Academy I'm surrounded by people who are much more expert: the Head of the course, Mary Hammond; Karen Rabinovitz and Julie Armstrong, both great choreographers; and my wonderful musical director, Andrew Friesner.

Lolly: You also help in the training of student musical directors at the RAM. What is your definition of a great MD?

George: Above everything they have to have an innate sense of the theatre, a good sense of voices, and a very strong sense of tempo, which is not as common as one might suspect. Nearly everybody is occasionally faster or slower than they think. Nigel Lilley, who is far from puritanical in his ways, is totally puritanical about not drinking before a show—even at lunchtime—because of wanting to set absolutely the right tempo. And, of course, with a wonderful MD in cabaret you can change the key or the tempo right until the day you open. You can't do that with musicals because the orchestration is already done.

There's a wonderful course for musical directors at the RAM, but it's led me to think that some of the piano teaching at the conservatoires is not good enough. When these students arrive, their playing is often too loud and too hard—as if they'd been brought up entirely on Bartok but not on Chopin. I spend a term saying, 'Not so loud!' and 'Please, may I tie your leg to the chair so we don't have the loud pedal all the time?'

Lolly: Do you ever work with the singers without your MD?

George: I might if I think someone's got a strange blockage. There may be a moment when someone finally hears the thing you've told them five times, and on a lucky day you may get somebody to have a different attitude about his or her voice. The problems may be very simple. They may consider consonants a regrettable necessity, or they may sing through commas or stop at meaningless points because that's what the music seems to tell them. You may only have to say to them, 'How would you say that?' or 'Look at the punctuation.'

Lolly: They learn the music but don't think about the meaning of the words.

George: And when they do that, they tend to do it uninflected. If you can get them to do big inflections, that often reveals the meaning. Get them to be specific and work as if they had no voice at all. Half of the material I use could be done equally well by people who aren't particularly good singers.

Lolly: Where do you find the material?

George: Someone once said rather breathily, 'It must take a lot of research.' It didn't take any research at all! I just know an awful lot of songs. And I suppose I'm keeping some of them alive.

Lolly: And you have sheet music for all of them?

George: Often I transcribe them from records. That's something I did at the BBC for *On the Bright Side.* I had a little caravan—before the present TV Centre was built—and we just sat and listened to the music and transcribed the songs. Writing a song down from a record, you'd often find a line that you couldn't quite decipher. You'd get secretaries in, you'd get actors in, and everybody would try to figure it out.

Lolly: You must have a great collection of recordings.

George: And a lot of it is irreplaceable. It became a status symbol in the '60s to have a recording of a Broadway show that hadn't opened yet in London. The radio wouldn't play a song until the show had opened here, so at 10:30 on opening night disc jockeys would play the music, but if any of your friends went to the States, they could bring you back a record. All that period had masses of little revues in New York, places like Upstairs at the Downstairs. About every four years Leonard Silman did a revue called *New Faces,* which is where Eartha Kitt had her first big success. In fact, *New Faces* was the first job that Maggie Smith had in the States.

Lolly: What happened to revue? There isn't much of it around these days, or am I just missing it?

George: Sometime in the '60s, around *Beyond the Fringe,* the critics collectively decided that they didn't want to see any revue again apart from terribly smart young men in black polo sweaters. The received version is that nobody wants to see it, but what frustrates me is that this doesn't reflect everybody's tastes. There are people who want to perform revue and there are audiences who want to see it.

The first years I went to New York, every time I went to the theatre we went out afterwards to places like Sweeney's or the Bakery or Michael's Pub. Now there's not much on offer apart from the Algonquin and the Café Carlisle, which cost and arm and a leg. Elaine Stritch did the Carlisle last year and she did entirely new material—she did nothing she had ever been associated with—and that takes nerve. Coward did an awful lot with her and she was always outrageous. He said, 'At the first night party, you have got to be restrained.' When she arrived in some very strange outfit, he said 'I didn't ask you to come as a fucking geography teacher!' Bram Lewis, who I stay with in NY, used to have a theatre in Westchester and he was very clever at getting people to do benefits. Stritch did a benefit for him, but the one thing she asked for was a car to take her from NY— and she made a 200-mile detour to visit her sister. Marvellous. Crazy!

But really, there are few places left that do cabaret. There are some on Restaurant Row like Don't Tell Mama, but even then those are only for try-out acts—somebody might do every second Sunday at 7 o'clock—but nobody does seasons. Erv Raible has started a venue in Staten Island and people go there from the city.

Erv runs the Cabaret Conference at Yale—he's a great talent spotter. Gary Lyons, who had been at Central, went there one year as a student and he introduced me to Erv, who then invited me there to teach every summer. It's such fun! Though we work all the time. The first weekend, we see the students perform and talk to them about their work, then on the Sunday evening we do this fearsome faculty performance for the public. I've done a medley of music hall songs, sometimes I do 'Don't Put your Daughter on the Stage', and last year I did a song I'd written about being at the Conference.

Lolly: You've written a lot of songs in your life.

George: I've written hundreds and they've all been performed, but they've all been site-specific for a short-lived show so I don't

"What best describes George? Him rushing in at 5 AM to wake me up: 'John, John! Listen and tell me if you think this is funny!'"

John Jones, Director, teacher

have a portfolio. I make the songs specific to the occasion so there's no reason to ever revive them.

Lolly: Do you still get performance nerves?

George: The scary thing at the Conference is not that you perform in the cabaret but that you really don't have any rehearsal time—terrifying, but very good for the soul. Most of the others don't bat an eye—people like Amanda McBroom are performing about thirty or forty weeks a year. She left the conference two days early one year because she was going to be performing somewhere vast with about 5,000 seats. Do you know Amanda McBroom's work? She's a terrific woman and a marvellous songwriter—she wrote 'The Rose'. She had always played the guitar and been a folk singer and one time she strummed something and said to her husband, 'Is this a song?' And he said, 'It's a song.' Then she was driving in her car and the whole lyric of 'The Rose' fell into her mind. She said to her husband, 'Do you think this is a song?' He said, 'I think you've just written a standard.'

On the first Saturday night two of the starry people do a show: one year it was Amanda McBroom and Julie Wilson. Another year it was Julie and Jason Graae. Jason is a wonderful comedian and a beautiful singer. He never stops working. It seems to me that every time they do new studio recording of a Kern or a Gershwin musical, Jason is on it. And Julie Wilson is still regarded as the queen of Broadway cabaret.

Julie is in her 80s and she's everything I love. She does her songs with such intensity and wit, and she is one of the most idealistic people I've ever met in the theatre. She's a life force coupled with such generosity. Every night she's not working herself, she's off seeing some young performer's new act and giving advice: 'Honey, you don't want to start with that

number!' Every one of the kids at Yale will be able to write
to her to say where they'll be appearing and she'll go to see
them. She once was appearing somewhere in a blizzard and
management said, 'We'll cancel.' She said, 'No. We'll see if
people come.' Two people arrived, so she did the whole show.
And they became lifelong friends.

Julie started as a seventeen-year-old hoofer and she's been in
the theatre for sixty-five years. When I first saw her, she was
playing Bianca in *Kiss Me, Kate* in London, then she stayed
and took over from Mary Martin in *South Pacific*. She used to
get a train to Brighton on Saturday night, book into a hotel,
talk to nobody on the Sunday, walk all the way to Rottingdean
where she had tea and walk all the way back. Monday she had
lunch, went back to London for a singing lesson, then went to
the theatre. A couple of years ago she came to give a talk to the
students at the Royal Academy and the most heartfelt thing she
said was, 'Girls, look after your feet. Take your pretty shoes in
a bag.' She still goes to her singing teacher: 'People talk about
money notes? I never had any.'

But she has such great wit and passion to communicate and
a passion to entertain—you understand every word she sings.
She has a long self-training in digging for the basic meaning of
a song and in drawing every phrase of it so that the meaning
of the song—emotionally and verbally—absolutely sizzles.
She chooses her material brilliantly and it all says something
she feels about life—frivolous or deep. One year she said to
a student 'Why do you do that song?' …'Because my music
teacher told me to and the arranger said it would be good.'
…'Do you like the song?' …'No.' …'Then don't do the
fucker!'

Julie was dazzlingly beautiful and always wore these very low-
cut gowns and then a few years ago a customer—somebody
she didn't know—said, 'I can't bear to look at those bones.' So
the low-cut gowns were all out. She uses a feather boa and she

"Everybody who goes to the Cabaret Conference goes out of a desire to learn and they have some quality, some ineffable thing, that is uniquely them that they long to express in music. Our job as teachers is to help that singer get everything out of the way that is impeding them from being themselves—not to tell them who they are, but to help them peel away affectations, habits, mannerisms, the things they hide behind. That takes great care. And that's why every year I beg to be teamed with George because he constantly models respect to the students. George and I like to listen and watch and wait. Sometimes you don't know what you're going to say until that silence. They finish their song and George will let it sit in the space for a moment. Then he begins. We both try to start with the thing that can be fixed in a short amount of time: the thing that will make a difference and will allow the student to have a real success. That may sometimes start a chain reaction that will fix a lot of other things, too, like a billiard ball hitting a ball that sends another ball into the pocket. If someone comes with a big vocal technique issue, we can't fix that in twenty minutes so why start there? People perhaps sometimes need to be reminded of what they do well, and then they need help with that thing that can be changed in this amount of time, and then they can go on to other transformations. George is very firm and very incisive, but he is not sharp with his comments. He offers suggestions and lets the students do the work. And he sometimes changes his mind. He's very positive with everyone and it really works! It's very easy to find people

always wears a gardenia, which is homage to Billie Holiday—she was a fan and a friend. Julie recently did four weeks in New York and she said, 'It's a rough life. You were a young girl and everybody said you were beautiful and all the guys were chasing you. Suddenly you're this old broad and you think, "Have I got a career yet?" The Metropolitan is a hot room, so if they offer it you'd better take it and hope it hasn't closed before you get there. And don't make waves.' So she did four weeks of Thursday through Sunday and she said, 'I got the notice of my life in the New York Times. I cried for three days.' The review was like a valentine.

Following a stroke and having all sorts of physical difficulties, Julie was talking to her sister who said, 'Aren't you done showing off yet?' And Julie just said, 'Nope.' She and Margaret Whiting, another cabaret legend, are like the history of American show business. And in a few years a lot of that will be gone. They are the aristocracy of a vanished world of smart supper clubs.

Lolly: Who else teaches at the conference?

George: It's a wonderful faculty. Sally Mays, a superb singer and actress, is at home in every style. Carol Hall, who wrote the Broadway hit, *The Best Little Whorehouse in Texas*, continues to write some of the most tender and yet witty songs I know. Tovah Feldshuh is a remarkable singer and Broadway performer, and a superlative teacher. And there is the wonderful, adorable Laurel Massé. I'm mad about her. She was one of the founding members of Manhattan Transfer, a terrific person and teacher—and a great solo performer. John says he's a little afraid we may run away together. Laurel and I have taught together a lot—we are so on the same wavelength—and we often work with Tex Arnold, who is a genius MD.

> who will throw tomatoes, but you need somebody who will celebrate your successes. George is a role model. The more I know him, the more of a role model he is for me."
>
> *Laurel Massé, Singer*

But then all of those MDs at Yale—Chris Denny, Paul Trueblood, Alex Rybeck, Rick Jensen—they are incomparable. You can give them an ordinary commercial copy of 'I Could Have Danced All Night' and say, 'I'd like it three tones higher and as a Samba,' and what you immediately get is an arrangement. And they know as much about lyrics as they do about music.

Tex and Pam Myers did a very grand cruise for three weeks where they did four performances. Pam teaches at Yale, too, and was in the original cast of *Company* and sang, 'Another Hundred People.' She told this great story about the second night when the second string critics came in. Out of sheer nerves and exhaustion Pam did the song half a tone higher than the band and she did it all out. At the end, somebody came up to her and said, 'I know Stephen Sondheim writes very dissonant music, but it's brilliant that you were able to do that. How did you ever learn it?' She didn't even know she'd done it!

Of course, I love all this. I'm such a show biz freak and the gossip at meals is just magic.

I worked with Margaret Whiting the first three or four times I did the Cabaret Symposium—before it was at Yale, when it was still at the O'Neill Center—and her anecdotes made my hair stand on end. Margaret is the daughter of Richard Whiting, who was a Hollywood composer in the '30s. She came in to see her father with a lollypop in her hand and he said, 'Don't get it sticky on my piano.' Out of that he came up with 'Good Ship Lollypop' for Shirley Temple.

Johnny Mercer, the great lyric writer, was Margaret's godfather and mentor and he and Harold Arlen called her 'The Kid'. They had written 'That Old Black Magic' and the singer who was going to do the recording was pregnant so they said, 'Let The Kid do it'. It made her something of a recording star. She said, 'The world had changed. But my contract hadn't. It was still $75 a side and no royalties.'

Margaret was considered not photogenic, so Judy Garland did the movies and Margaret did the recordings. Margaret once told me, 'I gave a party every Saturday night in Hollywood, but I always had just a few people for dinner first. This particular night I think it was Mel Tormé, Martha Raye, Judy Garland and Mickey Rooney. Johnny Mercer phoned and said, "Harold and I have just come up with a song. Do you want to hear it?" I said, yes! It was 'Blues in the Night', and Judy and I raced to the piano to see who could learn it first.' Now, that's what I call a party. I want to go to parties like that! Frank Loesser wrote 'Baby It's Cold Outside' for his wife and him to do at parties. The actress, Betsy Blair, was married to Gene Kelly at the time and she said people found out if the Loessers were free before they decided on a date for a party. Isn't that great? When I was a student, I remember George Devine saying, 'We went to a marvellous party at the weekend. Danny Kaye and John Gielgud improvised a sketch as a dentist and a patient, which was hysterical.' And I thought, 'I WANT TO BE THERE.'

Lolly: Does Margaret Whiting still teach at the conference?

George: No, she had a stroke and doesn't perform anymore either, but she still organizes the Johnny Mercer awards. She was married to a guy called Jack Wrangler who was a porn star in gay movies. He was very funny about it all: 'I'm appalled how they cleaned up New York. The Adonis on 8th is gone. That's where all my movies premiered!' Margaret was a huge recording star in the '30s and '40s and she's the history of Hollywood for all that period. It was 'Uncle Ira' Gershwin and 'Uncle Jerry' Kern.

"George is unique. His knowledge of the theatre is encyclopaedic and what I enjoy about him most is the incredible diversity of his enthusiasm: he is as excited by the intoxicating fizz of a Cole Porter lyric as sung by Mabel Mercer as he is by Olivier leading the troops at Agincourt. He has always remained aware and abreast of the shifting currents and changes in the theatre—that's why he's still young, I think—and he's an inspirational figure to many of us."

Matt Ryan, Director

And I can't get enough of those stories. The people at Yale are the very best of the best and I just love every minute of being there. The conversations in the dining room thrill me. Maybe somebody mentions 'Smoke Gets in Your Eyes' and we all know it was Jerome Kern, but then we have a very spirited conversation about who did the lyrics and what movie it came from. And somebody will know. I know material from American musicals and tiny revues from the '50s; and in England, apart from the director, Matt Ryan and Michael Chance, an ex-Central student that performs with me in cabaret, I never meet anyone who also knows all this material.

Lolly: It's like a support group…

George: …For the mentally deranged.

Lolly: And you introduce all those American cabaret artists to music hall?

George: I give a lecture about music hall every year. I play a lot of songs—either recordings or on the piano—and even if they never do the material, it's valuable for them to know that music

"George is inspiring, delightful and incredibly knowledgeable about every aspect of theatre, film and performance—from Chekhov to old time music hall—and one just trusted everything he taught you. His passion for all types and styles of performance was highly infectious and totally incurable and he was always more interested in practice than in theory. He had a huge collection of recordings of some of the most famous stand-ups, singers and comedians of the past; and he would play those records for us, so that we could get a feeling for timing and delivery and rapport with an audience, giving us the precious opportunity to 'watch, listen and learn' from the wings."

Cherie Lunghi, Actress

hall had a direct influence on the origins of the American musical.

Jerome Kern spent some time in the first decade of the 20th century in London and saw many of the great music hall people, and his collaborator early on was P. G. Wodehouse, who certainly inherited the music hall tradition.

Daisy Maybury had the 299-seat Princess Theatre in New York and she avoided all things Broadway. P. G. Woodhouse and Guy Bolton wrote a series of musicals for the Princess, with Wodehouse doing all the lyrics. The music was very integrated and—in absurdist Woodhouse terms—proper, silly, preposterous stories. In a way, Woodhouse was the inventor of the modern American lyric. Those musicals inspired people like Rogers and Hart, and Ira Gershwin.

First-generation Americans like Ira Gershwin and Yip Harburg were absolute disciples of Gilbert and Sullivan. Harburg, who wrote 'Buddy Can You Spare a Dime' and 'Over the Rainbow', started out in commerce, but when the depression came along he lost all his money. He said, 'I left the insane world of commerce and moved to the sanity of theatre.' Growing up, he and Gershwin were in neighbouring tenements and both of them were mad about light comic verse—twenty lines on a topical subject that were published in the newspapers then. Ira read a W. S. Gilbert lyric to Yip and Yip said 'There's music to that.' So he went home and got the phonograph and listened to Gilbert and Sullivan for the first time. It's fascinating, that interaction. The first act finales of Gershwin's musicals are really modelled on Gilbert and Sullivan.

Lolly: What else happens at the Yale conference??

George: After we've seen all the students over the first weekend, they are split into small groups and each group will have three hours with Laurel, Tex and myself, while other groups are with other faculty trios. We do everything from helping them to understand the meaning of the song, to their take on it, to their finding a different key or better tempo. Or maybe it's just changing the position of their bodies.

Lolly: Are you ever at a loss as to what to say?

George: It's something I fear all the time. On every song, on every speech. I work with singers or actors and every time they start I think, 'What am I going to say?' And I'm not alone. Sometimes you just have to get them to sing again because nobody can think of anything to say. And sometimes you have a reaction to their material that it is hard to get beyond. I've got such an objection to songs that try to make you a better human being and I can't tell you how strongly I feel about that.

We work very long hours, often until 10 PM. We go for drinks until midnight and I get up at 6 AM and go to the exercise room. I'm on such a high just being there with those people. Because I'm the only Brit, they think I'm cleverer and funnier than I actually am—which I'm not going discourage.

Really I'm spoiled from the second I set foot in America. It's very bad for my character to stay there any longer than I do.

"George Hall has always been, and continues to be, a complete and unending source of inspiration. His love of musical theatre and performers is legendary. I often see him at the theatre, after he has put in a long working day, doing what he loves best, supporting musical talent."

Sandra Caron, Actor, Author

"George's advice on what to say to someone after a questionable performance? 'Well, what about you then!'

Jessica Turner, Actress

People can't understand when I tell them that New York is my dream holiday. I stay with Bram Lewis. I wake up early, take hours over a shower and reading the NY Times, have a leisurely breakfast and a stroll into the park, read my book, go to the Met, read my book again, stroll home, have another shower, meet a friend and then go to the theatre or a cabaret. I never have a day like that in England. It doesn't matter if I want to have lunch at 11 or 2 or 3 or not at all. And the apartment is so restful. It's unbelievable. It's on 94th on the West Side, and it's like living on a little street in London in an earlier time. Last year not only did we not lock the door, we didn't *close* the door—so the cat could get in. Kids play on the street as if it were a small village. In New York! Imagine.

Lolly: When did you first go to New York?

George: I stayed there in 1975 on my way to the American Theatre Association Conference. That was a very strange event. I think American theatre is much less cluttered now than it was. People then were using a vocabulary that was all tied up with the Method and the Actors' Studio.

There was a pre-conference workshop in Baltimore, but the main events were in Washington, D.C. I was the guest speaker for the 'feast', which was a very curious name for an evening reception. They all thought I was going to talk about how dreadful the American theatre was and they were amazed when I expressed my great admiration for it. I also gave a talk about voice—and I was being very factual—but I got so many laughs, I felt like Jack Benny. Somebody asked some very po-faced question and I answered, 'Well, I think we do that so our acting is less boring.' I didn't mean it to be funny, but everybody laughed.

There were some fascinating people there, but a lot of it was absolutely nutty. At any moment during the conference there were six things on and there were indefatigable Americans determined to see them all—people came in for a sentence and a half. One of the talks was 'An Approach to Characterisation Through a Synthesis of Sexual Mechanics…and so on and so on'. Most of the talks had titles that were longer than the actual talk. There was another man who said he had found a way to solve all movement problems, which was that you lay on the floor with your head on this wooden thing. It was full of mad, mad people!

Lolly: Everyone looking for a method, a theory?

George: And you know that's not my thing.

I think I've learned more in my life by watching great performers than I've learned from anything else. Great singers, great dancers, great actors, great performers: Judy Garland, Margot Fonteyn, Edith Evans. Watching terrific performers is a better education—far better than theory. And I always encouraged students to see everything.

Lolly: You are continually seeing ex-students or colleagues or friends in productions. When I see someone I know, I find that I rarely get lost in a total transformation.

George: The most stunning transformation I've ever seen was Rosemary Harris in *Lost in Yonkers*. She's the gentlest, sweetest person, with the gentlest, genuine voice—and this harsh, domineering, nasty woman came out.

Lolly: Was Olivier always a little bit Olivier? Was Edith Evans always a little bit Edith Evans?

George: I know—a bit from hearsay—that Edith Evan's young career was full of amazing transformations. She didn't play anybody young until she was about thirty-five. Until then she played old crones. And she was nearly fifty when she played Rosalind. James Agate said of her, 'This huge variety of people—they all appear to have been Edith Evans.' Then maybe there's a point in time where somebody's options change or the persona becomes more stated.

Lolly: Or maybe it's an actor's choices in the parts they play?

George: Judi Dench does things that people beg her not to do. Peggy Ashcroft begged her not to do Lady Bracknell and she was stunning. The voice is so distinct, but the person isn't. Her Lady Macbeth was astonishing. I'm mad about physical and vocal transformation, perhaps more than most people. Remember that class I used to do about funny walks: walking with turned in feet, walking unevenly?

Lolly: And how that transforms you from the outside in, letting that create a character. Some people let it transform them; others want to put a cabaret act on top.

George: I've always found it terribly easy. If someone is walking oddly on the street and I walk that way—I feel like them. When Alec Guinness was a young actor he walked halfway across London following people and studying their walks. You could say that Alec Guinness was the greatest transformer, yet somehow in my book he's one rung below Gielgud, who wasn't such a great transformer.

Lolly: What's the difference between transforming into a different character and taking a character and translating it through your own creativity?

George: Your soul? In those early things—in *Great Expectations* and in *Kind Hearts and Coronets*—Alec Guinness was wonderful. Yet somehow he's not as exciting as Gielgud, who could never stop being recognizable. Gielgud had poetry and soul and depth.

What is interesting about Fonteyn—you can think that a lot of the ballerina parts are very like each other, all about lyricism and bravura—but she had a slightly different makeup for everything and there was a differentiation inside her about a character. When she first started she was desperate because she wasn't sure she could do the steps, but it was never difficult for her to believe she was a village maiden.

I find the great careers inspiring and very instructive. We did *Peer Gynt* at the Old Vic in 1961. Watching Wilfred Lawson rehearsing was fascinating because he did everything wrong. Not only didn't he speak Standard English, he spoke 'Wilfred Lawson English'. He played the Button Moulder and he didn't come on for three hours. Then when he came on he was slow and he didn't quite say the lines, and yet he was terrific. Leo McKern played Peer Gynt and in rehearsals he went over the top immediately, which was his way of making elbowroom. Everything was wild, mad, a free caricature. Then he would reduce it. Everyone works in a different way. It's personal to them and they might not be able to define it. Edith Evans used to say, 'If I knew what I was doing, maybe I couldn't do it.'

Lolly: Face it. Edith Evans was your favourite.

George: I once said to Dame Edith, 'I'm accused of running a fan club at Central for all of the people I adore—like you.' She said, 'Who are the others?' and was greatly relieved when I said Margot Fonteyn and Lena Horne—who were not actresses.

Lolly: What was Dame Edith like?

George: You know Bill Gaskill, the wonderful director who ran the Royal Court? He and I were talking about her and not only do we remember everything she said, but we remember the exact words she used—because everything turned out like an epigram. He told me that she had him to dinner and she said, 'I'm giving you a cheese. It's called Fromage Monsieur. I think you'll like it.' She said it as though she'd said something very witty, and it was the greatest commercial. We did a television play together and Avril Elgar and James Maxwell gave a party.

Edith was mixing the salad and she said, ' I was once told by a French woman that you should do this till your arms ache.' It's *how* she said those things that was so very funny. John and I still say that when we make a salad.

You just never knew if she was aware that these things were funny. She got nervous and stopped going out to dinner parties when she was playing Millimant because she could sense people thought she was going to say brilliantly witty things.

Edith was very religious. Peter Brook directed her in *The Darkest Light is Enough* and he told her, 'Enter and then count four before you…' and she said, 'My timing was given to me by God.' She thought she'd worked it all out with God: 'God was very good to me. He didn't send me on tour. I was so immature; I'd have got bad habits. I was only in the West End with Mary Gerald and Hubert Harven; and they had meticulous English and they picked me up on everything I did that was not right.' She lived in the Albany just near the Royal Academy in Piccadilly, which is mentioned in *The Importance of Being Earnest*. It's very grand and Edward Heath was one of her neighbours. She saw him getting into a cab and said to him in that wonderful voice of hers: 'Common vowels, Mr. Heath.'

But really, anything she said about acting was valuable. She said, 'Listen, but don't show you're listening.' Expressionless listening. I once asked her how she coped with a long run and she said, 'Well, it's no use waiting till 7:30. If it's been on a long time, about half way through the afternoon I say to myself, 'Edith, you are a very lucky girl because this evening you get to be somebody else.' And if she weren't in the first twenty minutes of the play, she'd listen from offstage and think: 'They are dull and need cheering up,' or 'They are bright and need calming down.'

Edith was famously mean with her money—John would go to collect her for some function at Central and she'd say, 'Will there be a sandwich?'—but she worked terribly hard, and when she was doing a part she paid someone to come in to hear her lines at home. I remember when we did *Time Remembered* there was a line she just could not remember. I was with Michael Elliott when she said, 'Now if he could just stand there, and if she was over there…'. Then she moved the two actors around about a couple of inches. 'Now I shan't forget it again.' And she never did. Michael said to me as we were leaving, 'Now that is fine-tuning'. But people found her very tiresome because, say, an actor's tie got stained and he got a different tie, or if he was going to part his hair in a different way, he had to go to her dressing room to tell her. Because it threw her.

I'm thrilled to have worked with her on *Hay Fever*. I adored her and I'd always worshipped her work. It was a marvellous cast, with George Devine, Paul Eddington, Pamela Brown. Maggie Smith was the flapper. Edith had it in her contract that from day one that we had to have the proper furniture. At the rehearsals, everybody went off for lunch and she would stay in the rehearsal room with a sandwich. She just got very accustomed to the height of the chair, the sofa—then in a curious way she wasn't nervous on the transmission. She said, 'Georgie, this is not rehearsing, this is what I call practice.' It's funny, only two people have called me Georgie in my life: Edith Evans and Laurence Olivier.

Lolly: How did you meet Olivier?

George: I knew Joan very well, and a friend and I were at her flat for supper. Olivier rang and Joan said, 'He's coming round.' I now think he was as nervous of meeting her contemporaries as we were of meeting him. He was going through a wild phase of being mad about colonic irrigation and he nervously launched into that topic and described everything in minute detail. It was so funny. I thought: a) I never thought I'd meet him and

b) I didn't think our conversation would be entirely about his bowel movements.

Lolly: So you knew that he and Joan were seeing one another?

George: There were the rumours, of course, but I knew. I remember Joan ringing one night for me to come round—she was in Irvington Square and I was in Cadogan Square, which was just a step away: 'There's a car gone round the square for ages and I think they're trailing me.' I went over and we got a cab to a pub, went in and then out a different door. It was ridiculous. Equally, Olivier said then that if you weren't a publicity seeker they didn't really go after you. I think he was right, because all Fleet Street knew it was happening and they didn't say a word. There was a theatre columnist on the Evening News who said to Joan rather cryptically, 'Tell your friend not to park so close.' If either of them had been people who had been using the press for self-promotion, I'm sure they would have been persecuted. They were being followed, but very little ever got printed. It came as a total surprise to everybody.

Sir Laurence could make himself unrecognisable. I don't mean he did disguises, but by that time he wore really pretty terrible business suits and he could blend into a crowd very easily. People said that at the height of his fame, when Olivier and Leigh took their Old Vic tour of Australia and New Zealand, mayors and public officials took it as a dress rehearsal for the arrival of the Queen. It was all very glittery. Then when he went to Scunthorpe to see Joan's parents, they sat around the piano singing Gilbert and Sullivan and it was like an escape to a different life for him.

I worked with him when he was doing *Lear* for television: 'I'm old and I'm tired, but I've got to be able to yell in this part. Everybody says we can do that with the microphone. No, I've got to be able to yell.' But really, he knew his voice inside out and didn't need me at all. I think he needed the equivalent of a pacer, like a runner needs a competitor. We worked on text, but we never went beyond the storm scene: 'That's me now. For the rest of it I don't have to do any work.' He did have a great deal of neck and shoulder tension, but he'd try anything. I remember being irritated when some student at Central would say, 'I think that's a silly exercise,' when Olivier would say, 'Try anything.' And you knew he would. He was astounding and his voice was marvellous. He bumped his elbow into a little commedia del arte figurine, and in mock rage he went 'aaaarrrrghhh', and it made my hair stand on end. But he said things that would alarm a speech therapist: 'If my voice feels a bit tired, I treat it harshly. I yell.'

Working with him, I discovered the operative word was 'effective'. If you said, 'That feels more real,' it didn't hit him in the same way as, 'That was terribly effective.' Very telling. I was terrified, I had to gulp to knock on the front door, but I loved working with him. He tired very easily, so he'd say, 'I think we'll stop and have a cup of coffee and a chocky bicky.' Then the anecdotes would start.

One day he went to make coffee and he came back singing, 'Georgie baby, da da da dee dee,' and he said 'What is that?' I told him, 'That's a very obscure Rogers and Hart song from a film called *You're the Cats*.' And he said, '*You're the Cats*. Yes, Ben Lyon and Ona Munson. Noël and I were in New York— we were sharing a flat when we were doing *Private Lives*—and

> "George has the Twinkle Factor— which always makes him fun to be around—but his concerned caring is always as evident as his good humour. On his last visit to NYC, I was bemoaning the express speed of passing years and the usual worries of maturity. He lent across the table to confide, 'Darling, some of my best jobs came after I passed my 80th!' As usual, he made me laugh. For him, becoming 80 was just the start of another adventure. Apart from all the technical skills George modestly offers, his continual encouragement and delight in living have been valuable influences. His wonder at life is a great lesson on enjoying the moment—a necessary philosophy for anyone in Show Biz."
>
> *Marion Sybil Lines, Actress*

we went to see that movie in the afternoon. Noël was so clever, he came home and sat at the piano and he could immediately do the lyrics and the music.' Of course, those stories were thrilling for me.

And he had a grim sense of humour. Esmond Knight was in *King Lear*, and Esmond was blind. Leo McKern was in it, and Leo had a glass eye. Something had happened to Sir Laurence's eye and he said, 'It's like a blind convention.'

He was very sweet when he got frail, but I don't think he was particularly easy. Once when Joan was away, he and Tamsin were the only people at the Chelsea flat. Tamsin was at Central, and he phoned the school and said he had to talk to her. The receptionist told him, 'We're not allowed to get people out of class,' and he said, 'But this is very important.' When Tamsin came to the phone he said, 'Darling, how about lamb chops tonight?' Wonderful.

Lolly: He and Noël Coward were obviously great friends.

George: There's a wonderful Coward story and only recently Richard Olivier said that he was the little boy. The Oliviers used to live on the seafront in Brighton and there's a place for blind servicemen along the way called St. Dunstan's. Coward took Richard for a walk and they saw two dogs copulating. Richard asked, 'What are they doing?' and Coward said, 'Well, the first dog has gone blind and the other one is very kindly pushing him to St. Dunstan's.'

Coward was as funny in life as he was in his writing. Somebody asked him, 'Are you superstitious?' and he said, 'I try to avoid thirteen in bed.' Isn't that the best? There was an evening paper in Sydney, Australia, called The Star and a reporter once said to Coward, 'Have you a word for The Star?' and he replied, 'Twinkle.'

Lolly: Were Olivier and Gielgud friends?

George: When Olivier did *Richard III*, Gielgud gave him one of his most valuable possessions, which was the sword that Edmund Kean had used as Richard III. But I think they were uneasy with one another. To me, Gielgud was the top of the profession. There was humility to him as an actor, yet he accused himself of egomania all the time: 'I'm totally self-absorbed. I'm not interested in anything but the theatre.' He endlessly listed his faults as an actor: 'I couldn't move and I never had the physicality that Olivier had.'

Gielgud's mother was one of the Terry sisters but she wasn't an actress, so he was Ellen Terry's nephew. He first walked on with three lines at the Old Vic, and one of the Terry family actors took him aside and said, 'You mustn't go on with this. You cannot do it. You're hopeless.' Yet I think his turned into one of the great careers. Someone once said he had a 'thirst for quality'.

Lolly: I recently saw a personal scrapbook that included two letters from Gielgud about a play that had been submitted to him. The first was a very genteel and polite, 'Thank you for the script. I look forward to reading it,' and the second was, 'This is the worst script I've ever read in my life! What makes you think you can write?'

George: His tactlessness was legendary. Margaret Leighton said she bumped into him when she was going for an audition and he said, 'Oh, fascinating part. I hope Hermione Gingold gets it.' He didn't censor anything he said; he just said it. With his OUDS production of *Romeo and Juliet*, Peggy Ashcroft and Edith Evans were the guest artists and he said, 'Two actresses the like of whom I hope never to work with again.' And there is a famous story of his being at the Ivy and talking to the playwright Edward Knoblock. He said, 'Oh god, have you ever met anyone so boring as Edward Knoblock? Oh! I mean the *other* Edward Knoblock.'

Lolly: And he was never embarrassed by it?

George: Apparently not. And then, on the other hand, Maggie Smith can make embarrassing stories so very funny. She once told me about the first time she met Coward and she went puce with embarrassment even remembering it. She was in *New Faces* of 1960-whatever, both here and on Broadway. For the finale they had elbow length gloves, very stylish. One of the buttons on her gloves had come off so the wardrobe lady had hastily sewn it. Coward was in and she was sent word that he was waiting for her. She tried to take off her glove, but she couldn't get it all the way off. Then she stepped on the hem of her dress. So she arrived bowed and with five drooping fingers!

On that same trip, Rogers and Hammerstein were about to do their television production of *Cinderella* and they wanted to see Maggie for it. The audition was in a hotel room, so she sang for them there and she could see they were less than impressed. They said, 'Thank you very much,' she opened the door to leave and she walked into the broom cupboard. She thought, 'I'm never coming out. I'm going to stay here for the rest of the night.' They had to come and rescue her. I relish funny stories forever.

Lolly: Are your favourites all theatre stories from theatre people?

George: Absolutely not! There is a wonderful friend of ours, a Yorkshire woman, who went to some swimming classes at the local pool. She was rather nervous about it so the instructor said, 'Look, I've got this rope here. You hold it and if you get nervous, just give it a little tug.' Well, of course, she did get nervous and she did give it a little tug. And she pulled the woman into the pool! I can wake at two in the morning and think about that and start laughing. It has never ceased to collapse me. Another one is a story about Margaret McCully, who worked with me at Central. She was sitting at the hairdressers with a hairdryer on and the woman next to her had her hairdryer on and was writing a letter. Margaret was looking over her shoulder at what she was writing and the woman wrote, 'I'm stopping writing now because the woman next to me is reading this.' And Margaret couldn't get away. She was stuck under that hairdryer!

Lolly: Do you have favourite plays that make you laugh?

George: I love a great deal of Alan Bennett, but I suppose John and I revere Neil Simon more than any other playwright around in the British theatre at the moment. Do you know the female version of *The Odd Couple*? The scene with the Spaniards is one of the funniest scenes in theatre. Bliss. I've done *Little Me* twice and the script is glorious. Everybody tries to say Simon is all about one-liners. Well, people used to say that about Oscar Wilde—as though one-liners are awfully easy. The most offensive phrase is when people say 'mere entertainment', which implies that if they stooped so low they could entertain you as well. Thank you! It's not easy to entertain people. Mere entertainment? There's nothing 'mere' about it.

Lolly: Entertainment. Long may it continue.

George: Absolutely. Kitty Carlisle died recently, at something like age 96. One of the musical directors at Yale was a great friend and went on holidays with her. A couple of years before she died, they went to Ireland and there was a place to make a wish on some stone. He couldn't resist asking Kitty what her wish was and she said, 'More of the same.' Isn't that marvellous, at age 96 or whatever?

But then, I find the age thing very curious. Did you know that once you're over 79, you're not considered a risk at airports? I was coming back from New York last year and at security everyone with British passports were told to go stand in a special line. Then this guard said, 'Wait, how old are you? No, you can just go through over there.' I thought, 'Wait a minute. I could blow this place up just as competently as anybody.'

Lolly: You don't seem old to me.

George: Well, in the theatre we're encouraged to grow old disgracefully.

Lolly: What do you see yourself doing next?

George: 'More of the same.' My career has gone from crazy showbiz, to *King Lear*, to Michael Elliott, to teaching all these very talented people. I'm very lucky. It's all been so 'untidy', as Michel said. Bizarre. **"**

Above Left: George's mother, Ann Hall, 1920s.
Above Right: Father, William Hall, WWI.

Below Left: George, age 1, with his parents, 1926.
Below Right: George, age 4, with his mother, 1929.

Above: George, age 14, back row, second from left,
George Heriot's School, Edinburgh, 1939.

Above Left: George, far left, front, Bombay, 1945.
Above Right: Pete, Doug, George, Geoff, Air Force, Austria, 1946-47.

*'I went to Paris for the first time in my life with George and some friends from the drama
school. It was wonderful. He was such fun on those trips!' Joan Plowright*

Above Left: (left to right) Joan Plowright, George Hall, Maureen Quinney.
Above Right: Ida Goldapple, Joan Plowright & George Hall, Paris, Easter 1950.

Left: George Hall, 1950s.
[Donald Southern]

Right: George's headshot, 1951,
includes information on the back:
Age 26, Height 5'8¹ᐟ²" [David Sim]

'I've never been 5'8¹ᐟ²" tall in my life.'

Above: *Country Cousins* (left to right) Mike Morgan with banjo, George Hall at the piano and Cilla Morgan, 1952.

Below: Eric Thompson, (Sophie & Emma's father) as William Corder.
Maria Marten, or Murder in the Red Barn
Frank Dunlop (Director), Richard Negri (Designer) George Hall (Music). Piccolo Theatre Company, Chorlton-cum-Hardy and Cambridge Arts Theatre, 1953-54.

Above Left: *Maria Marten, or Murder in the Red Barn.* (left to right, standing) Phyllida Law (Maria's mother), Ivo Roderick (Maria's father), Rosalind Knight (Maria's sister Anne), Mike Morgan (Tim Bobbin) John Roberts (Tober Sloper), (back row, right)Bernard Cribbins.

Above Right: *The Green Room Show,* (left to right) Bernard Cribbins, Andrée Melly, Annie Leake, Roger Cage, George Hall at piano, Edinburgh Festival, Pleasance Church Hall, 1954.

Below: *You and Your Wife* by Denis Cannan, directed by Frank Dunlop. Alan Bates' first professional engagement after RADA. Alan Bates (second from left), George Hall (third from left) Midland Theatre company, Coventry, 1955.

Above Left: George as Balthazar in *The Comedy of Errors,* 1955.
Above Right: George in *The Lark* by Jean Anouilh
Midland Theatre Company, Coventry, 1955.

Above: George Hall as Malachi Stack in *The Matchmaker* by Thornton Wilder
Midland Theatre Company, Coventry, 1955.

'I didn't have my own nose in the theatre for about 3 years!'

Above: *The Comedy of Errors* (left to right) James Cullerford, Bernard Kilby, Tessa Webb, George Hall, Midland Theatre Company, Coventry, 1955.

Above: *On the Bright Side,* BBC-TV, 1958 & 1959.
Back (left to right): Bob Stevenson, Amanda Barrie, and far right, Una Stubbs
Front (left to right): Sid Lotterby (floor manager), Douglas Squires, David Kernon, Stanley Baxter, James Gilbert (director), Betty Marsden, Eira Heath, Pip Hinton, Richard Warring, and George Hall

Above: *The Magistrate* by Arthur Wing Pinero.
George Hall (director), Clare Jeffery (designer)
First show to be designed for Central, Averham, 1964.

Above: Tom Courtney (centre) as Hamlet for Theatre 69 (Royal Exchange Theatre)
& Edinburgh Festival 1968.
Litz Pisk (movement), George Hall (music), Michael Elliott (director)

Above Left: *Movement and Sound,* George teaches the pavane. Martin Potter, front right, and behind him, Nigel Terry. Above Right: Black Death, (left to right) Jane Roberts, Steven Bradley, Vanessa Riches, Bob Booth (Cherie Blair's uncle) [Photo courtesy of CSSD]

Above: *Movement and Sound,* in class, 1965. [Photo courtesy of CSSD]

Above: *Giroflé – Girofla* by Charles Lecocq, directed by George Hall
Pat Heatley & Mickey Feast, 1967. [Photo courtesy of CSSD]

Above Left: Gloria Connell, *Giroflé – Girofla*, 1967. [Photo courtesy of CSSD]

Above Right: Zoe Wanamaker as Titania in *A Midsummer Night's Dream,*
Wimbledon School of Art, 1969. (Designer Philip Cox) [Photo: R.E. Brown printed
by permission of Wimbledon School of Theatre Design, Wimbledon College of Art]

Above: *Guys and Dolls,* Trevor Peacock (Nathan Detroit) & Zoe Wanamaker (Miss Adelaide) Theatre 69 (Royal Exchange Theatre), 1972.

Ring Round the Moon by Jean Anouilh
David Terence (director), Nic Ede (designer)

Above Left: Ralph Lawson, Cherie Lunghi. [Photo courtesy of CSSD]
Above Right: David Fielder, Sandra Dickinson, 1973.
[Photo: Peter Hudson, Photo courtesy of CSSD]

Above: Gala Evening, Central School of Speech and Drama.
(left to right) Norman Collins, Central School Chairman of Board of Directors,
Princess Alexandra, George Hall, Joanna Llyod, 1971. [Photo courtesy of CSSD]

Above: *Bluebeard* designed by Rich Croft. (left to right) Julia North, Sian Thomas,
Lindsay Duncan, Penelope Darch, Deborah Dennison. [Photo: R.E. Brown printed
by permission of Wimbledon School of Theatre Design, Wimbledon College of Art]

Above: George, Room B, Central – 1972. George has been teaching singing and musicality for over six decades. [Photo: John Ford, Photo courtesy of CSSD]

Above Left: Kate Nelligan & George in Room B
[Photo: John Ford, Photo courtesy of CSSD]

Above Right: Debroah Grant '67 teaches make-up to Kate Nelligan '72.
George often invited ex-students back to teach at Central.
[Photo: John Ford, Photo courtesy of CSSD]

Above Left: Central dressing room, early 1970s. [Photo courtesy of CSSD]
Above Right: American Theatre Conference, Baltimore, Maryland USA, 1975.
"I got so many laughs, I felt like Jack Benny."

Above: *Kiss Me, Kate,* directed by George Hall,
Central School of Speech & Drama 1975.
(left to right) Mark Lewis, Jessica Turner, Kevin Whateley, John Parsonson
[Photo courtesy of CSSD]

Above: George's last production of *Maria Marten, or Murder in the Red Barn*
Central, 1981. [Photo courtesy of CSSD]
(left to right) Francine Morgan, Lolly Susi, Jackie Lye, Alan (Scottie) Stewart

Above: *Au Revoir, George,* 5 April 1987.
Dame Vanessa Redgrave, George, Dame Peggy Ashcroft

Above: For George's retirement from Central in 1987, colleagues, friends and ex-students contributed toward the purchase of a white baby grand piano.

Above: John Jones and George Hall have been partners for over forty years.

The following is taken from George's lectures on music hall, given at the Cabaret Symposium at the O'Neill Center in 1998 and the Cabaret Conference at Yale in 2007.

If you were to ask the British to do quick associations and said 'cabaret', they might say: 'sophistication, elegance, Cole Porter, upper class'. If you said 'music hall', they'd say: 'raucous, noisy, vulgar, working class.' And I'm sure in today's world it doesn't seem immediately relevant. Oh, but it is!

Music hall is one of the tributaries that flowed into the amazing art form that is the Broadway musical—which is one of the great inventions in the world's theatre history. There are several periods in the history of the theatre when the theatre is at its most powerful—when a single event simultaneously attracts the intelligentsia, the middlebrows and the man in the street—when there aren't small esoteric audiences but instead the broad population being addressed. It happened in the ancient Greek theatre, it happened in the Elizabethan theatre, and I think it happened in the glorious days of the American musicals. Look at all of the components that went into creating that phenomenon: some came from France, Eastern Europe and the cantors, some came from the Blues, some came from the Viennese and Parisian operetta, some came from Gilbert and Sullivan. And an important strain came from the English music hall.

Music hall had very humble beginnings. Until the beginning of the 19th century, Britain was mostly rural. When people wrote new, funny or popular songs and brought them to market days and fairgrounds, everyone would learn a new song. Then the Industrial Revolution happened and it became an urban country, with all the money in mining and textiles and factories. It was the unacceptable face of capitalism: terrible, dreary towns, with row after row after row of indistinguishable houses. People had a very hard life, and it was quite normal to start work at 8:00 AM and finish at 10:00 PM with maybe one day off a year. It was a hard existence and a huge loss of identity for people. If you'd worked in a farm in the beginning of the 19th century, it may have been practically the feudal system but you knew the name of the people you worked for, and they knew your name. Suddenly there were faceless factory owners with a very cold attitude to labour. I think the way people coped was to create and perform songs that reflected their everyday real lives in highly coloured terms. French vaudeville was melodrama and tragedy; the Central European tradition was political; but the English tradition was about presenting your own life in front of you, larger than life. The songs are all terribly specific; they're hardly ever abstract; they're occasionally inspirational. The really great ones are about particular people: Harry or Joshua or somebody who's a husband, a chimney sweep or a railway driver.

It's wonderful the way accident plays its part in theatre history. Initially, the entertainer was somebody in the corner of the pub: 'Fred' was a great singer who'd had a few drinks, and he stood up and did a funny song and everybody laughed. The change from that to professional entertainment was simply that astute landlords realised that if you put a little platform in the corner of the pub with a piano and employed somebody to sing funny songs, you sold more beer. This is the impulse behind all music hall and all cabaret. And for a very long and happy time, people were able to drink and listen at the same time. They didn't have to have a two-drink minimum because I think if they'd had a twenty-two maximum it might have been a rather better idea. Drink was very, very cheap, so people rolled into work at 8:00 AM, pissed out of their heads. But then, England has a great tradition, which I think we've bequeathed to America, of feeling that if anyone is having a good time it should be put to a stop, so various regulations were brought in making it not permissible anymore to sell liquor in the same place as the entertainment. You started to have the entertainment place as an addition to the pub, and it evolved so that the entertainment place became big and the pub became the bar attached to it. The first time anyone custom-built a house for these shows was in 1852. One particular pub owner sold his bowling alley—they were very hot on bowling alleys at that time—and he turned it into a custom-built theatre. And he was the first person to charge admission. Instead of being a bit of free entertainment and we hope you drink more, it became somewhere you lined up and bought tickets and went into. Out of this evolved the extraordinary thing called 'music hall'.

It is unimaginable how many custom-built buildings there soon were for music hall. You didn't have to go very far—the theatres were in the suburbs as well as the city centre. At the turn of the century there were very nearly five hundred music hall theatres in Greater London alone, and they all played twice nightly. Think about it. A thousand audiences per evening left their homes to go to music hall.

If you've ever heard *Gypsy*, you know that terrible little corny orchestra that plays at the beginning. Most music hall bands sounded like that. They were frightful. They were grocers and plumbers who'd stopped their day job. And they only knew two tempi: too fast and too slow. But whatever bands did, performers didn't dare say anything—they were totally at their mercy. People like the Scottish Will Fyffe had a different costume and makeup for the different acts they did, so the audience would wait while a quick change happened with nothing much happening but the orchestra playing.

Yet some things about music hall were remarkably sophisticated. You know in Sondheim you often hear a word that hasn't got a rhyme to it and it finds its rhyme: 'Beauty celestial, the best you'll agree,' and that final recognition of rhyme is part of the joke. That playing with language and inventing trick rhymes comes from the music hall.

In music hall songs, everything is a story. Apart from musical theatre and cabaret—or Rap, which is something people listen to but don't go about whistling—few of our popular songs today are about anything except the two Ls: love and lust. Maybe you've got a more lucky life than I, but only a few minutes of my life per day are devoted to these subjects. The rest of the time I'm thinking about shopping or do I have to do the laundry. And we rarely reflect any of these in our popular songs. But the music hall was full of songs about work places, about family relationships, about mothers-in-law. They sang quite a lot about food. There are a lot of songs about drink—the downfall of the working classes. Gin, which was very cheap, was called 'mother's ruin', and there's a lovely song about a lady who overindulges in everything, called 'Don't Have Any More, Mrs. Moore'. The first verse is about how she has too many children. The next is about how she's had too many husbands. The third is as she's reeling out of the pub, and then into the chorus: 'Too many double gins give the ladies double chins'. That's one of the great music hall couplets.

The songs are all about humanity, about real human problems. There's a lovely one about a man who's encouraging his friend to get married:

> *'arry, 'arry, 'arry, 'arry.*
> *Now's the time for you to marry.*
> *A nice little widow with a nice little pub.*
> *Plenty of beer and 'baccy, plenty of grub.*
> *I'll go round to see you and keep you company.*
> *Wouldn't it be nice for her and you.*
> *Wouldn't it be nice for me.*

There's another one that's very sweet, about the young woman who's taken by her boyfriend to meet his mother: 'When he'd introduced me to his mother, she gave me such a cross-examination. Then she shook her head, looked at me and said: "Poor John, poor John".'

And music hall audiences were very noisy. The best way to control a noisy and rowdy audience is to tell them they are allowed to be noisy and rowdy at certain points. In many songs there was a form in which the performer told the story and then there was a very easily learned verse, which the public quickly picked up. Then they had to shut up to know what the next bit of story was before they were allowed to join in and get rowdy again. An archetypal one is called *Joshua*. The refrain says:

> *'Joshua, Joshua, why don't you call and see mama.*
> *She'd be pleased to know you are my best beau.'*

You sort of know there aren't rhymes in English for Joshua. So, it goes on:

> *'Joshua, Joshua, nicer than lemon squash you are.*
> *Yes, by gosh you are, Josh-u-osh-u-a.'*

The other thing that is typical: you have a quite meandering and complex tune and a lot of story, then you have a very easy chorus that a drunk lunatic can pick up in one hearing. Of course, then the lyric writers skill consists of writing a last bit of verse that leads into the chorus.

Joshua courted Miss May—
To be correct, I should say
She courted him, for he was so shy—
Dare not say 'Boo' although no one knew why.
They walked out for months and for months
But he never asked her to wed.
They'd sit hand in hand where the soft shadows fall –
He's sit there for hours and say nothing at all
Till one night May blushingly said,

'Joshua, Joshua, why don't you call and see Mamma?
She'd be pleased to know you are my best beau.
Joshua, Joshua, nicer that lemon squash you are,
Yes, by gosh you are Josh-u-osh-u-ah.'

Joshua said he would call
But never meant to at all.
He'd never met May's loving mamma
But he'd heard something of what mammas are!
Each night he saw May to her gate
But never would venture inside.
He'd give her a kiss and he'd wish her goodnight,
Then quicker than thought he would vanish from sight
Whenever May lovingly cried,

'Johua, Joshua' etc.

They met a lady one day.
'Oh, look there's Mother!' said May.
Joshua stared—said May, with a sigh,
'She is my step-mamma, younger than I.'
The couple were soon introduced.
He gazed with surprise at Mamma
Perhaps he preferred her, perhaps lost his head,

But Joshua married the mother instead,
And May never sings to her Pa

'Joshua, Joshua, why don't you call and see Mama….'

And so it goes on. That's tells you quite a lot about the shape and the character of what these occasions must have been like. You don't have to have a good voice; you don't have to do anything except tell the story. Many of the great stars of the music hall did not have what you might call 'a voice'. The greatest of them probably didn't know on any particular occasion whether they'd just sung or spoken the last line. They were concerned with communicating, with getting the song over. It is very naïve and simple material, not sophisticated, not satirical. It is not saying: 'Have you noticed how funny those other people are?' They celebrate how funny they are. There was a tall, gawky lady called Nellie Wallace, and there was big, fat lady called Lily Morris, and they were celebrating their oddity. The real subject matter was: 'Come and join me in my foolishness.'

Music hall entertainers had a huge ability to engage audiences. And audiences were tough. If you played Glasgow on a Saturday night, they used to say, 'Keep moving'—if they didn't like you, they threw things. Remember, there was no television, no movies. You did your song and if it was a success a year later you came back to Liverpool or Glasgow and people wanted to see you do the same song. Performers did a great deal of the same material for years and years. This makes for two possibilities: 1) you are totally stale and on automatic pilot, which I guess most of them were, or 2) if you are a genius, you will have honed that material to perfection. When I was a drama student I saw someone called Ella Shields. She was from Boston, Massachusetts, and had married an Englishman. A song was written for her called 'Burlington Bertie from Bow'. Now, everyone knew about Burlington Bertie. He was a very grand West End man-about-town, a character sung about by Vesta Tillie, who was a very famous male impersonator in wonderfully tailored clothes. 'Burlington Bertie from Bow' was the East End version of the same thing: a working class person of pretensions with frayed cuffs and cast off clothing, who hadn't two pennies to rub together but who put on a great act of airs and graces. In 1914, Ella Shields started singing the song 'Burlington Bertie from Bow' and forty years later she was still singing the same song. I saw her do it in 1950 and it was peerless perfection. There was a whole chorus where the band played, and she took off her top hat and simply polished it—an act of total authority and total poise.

Performers lives then were extraordinary. All the acts were solo acts. Through a quirk in the law you didn't have double acts, as duets might be regarded as a 'dramatic presentation', which you were only allowed to do in theatres that didn't sell alcohol. So apart from acrobatic troupes or mime troupes, all the acts were solos. People didn't do long spots. Mostly they did ten minutes: if you were a star you did fifteen. This was one of the blissful things of the music hall and variety—if you hated the performer, they were only on for ten minutes and maybe somebody absolutely great is going to come on next. In London I go to Fringe plays that may have only three characters and sometimes after ten minutes I hate them all—and I'm stuck there for the next two hours.

There was such demand for a star's services that if you were someone like Marie Lloyd you'd start the evening doing the first house at 6:15 PM at the first theatre, say the Holborn Empire, and you would be early on the bill. She'd do ten minutes and then get in the hansom cab waiting at the stage door, which would take her the Queen's Theatre, Shoreditch. She'd do ten minutes there. Another cab would take her to the Finsbury Park Empire, and she'd do ten minutes. Then they'd take her back to where she'd started to do the second house at 8:40, and she'd do the whole thing again. So it went on: six shows a night. You had to have three band parts, one for each of the theatres. And it's unimaginable now, too, that you could rely on getting through London traffic. If you tried to do that today, theatre managers would have heart attacks within three months.

The first year I was out of drama school I did a variety act—music hall became known as variety in the 1920s. I couldn't wait to shed my classical training and do what remained of variety in England, which at that time was in its very, very last days. I think you can say it died the year I did it: I hope the two things aren't linked. By 1952, variety was becoming strippers, becoming hideous, but I never regretted doing it. I met a very old couple that had worked for Fred Karno, where Stan Laurel and Charlie Chaplin started. Fred Karno was a great music hall impresario in the early 20th century. These two old performers were wonderful, and they told me about how before the First World War you had your engagement book filled up for a year or eighteen months ahead—the way opera singers do now: 'In fifteen months you're playing the Grand in Chatham'. It was a very different world.

What were some of these performers like? Well, the performers nearly always were working class people—the boy or the girl who is extrovert and likes entertaining suddenly becomes a professional entertainer. Careers were extraordinary. Marie Lloyd was one of the greatest. She was called the Queen of the Music Hall, and if I tell you about her, I tell you about music hall.

We're apt to think that instant stardom for teenagers started with Rock 'n Roll. Marie Lloyd started in the late 19th century at the age of fifteen and by the next year she was a big star making maybe £200-300 week. Imagine what that was in terms of today's money. She made a fortune: she lost a fortune. She had an archetypal star's life—rather like Garland and Piaf. She had a lot of lovers, three husbands who spent all her money, and she died at no great age and had that kind of Rudolph Valentino/Princess Diana funeral where half of London lined the streets to see her cortege. When she was a young performer, she was very pretty and she carried a little cane, and her early songs are very pert and sexy, saucy and provocative. Then she grew into being a real old bag and her later songs were about how she was an old bag among the ruins. The people who praised her were very unexpected—author and cartoonist, Max Beerbohm and perhaps most surprisingly, the poet T. S. Elliot—and everybody describes how she was simultaneously broad and delicate: big enough to get to the back of the gallery and yet very understated. She only worked into her 50s, when she did songs like 'A Little of What You Fancy Does You Good' with great innuendo.

Marie Lloyd had endless trouble with the London County Council. There's one story I love and I hope it's true. She used to sing a song: 'I Sits Among the Cabbages and Peas'. The LCC found this totally impermissible, so she changed it to 'I Sits Among the Cabbages and Leeks'. She kept being hauled up in front of her betters. They thought the lyrics of her songs would demoralize the working classes because they were so rude, but really it was all innuendo. She was able to make everything sound filthy. On one occasion the LCC had her up on a charge of being too rude, so she went into the court and was able to sing her songs so blamelessly that no one could see why there was a problem. Then she sang Tennyson's 'Come into the Garden, Maud' with such alluring innuendo that strong men paled. In 1912, the country decided to have what they chose to call a Royal Command Performance, which meant that by so-called command of the then King and Queen there was a great Variety Performance. Marie Lloyd was not invited because she was thought to be much too rude, so that evening she played at another London theatre and had a bill that said 'This Performance, like all Marie Lloyd's Performances, is by Command of the Great British Public'.

Music hall also had a lot of male impersonation. There was no female impersonation except in what we call Pantomime—a Christmas entertainment—but there was a lot of male impersonation. Another music hall artist, Hettie King, played a sailor on leave. She had a cigarette, and she lit a match, and then before the match reached the cigarette she remembered something she wanted to tell you. The audience always waited for the match to burn her fingers and it never did. The business was so polished. Vesta Tilly, the original Burlington Bertie, was included on the bill of the Command Performance but Queen Mary ostentatiously turned her back on the stage when she was on. She couldn't be seen looking at a woman wearing trousers. It was another world.

In the history of the feminist movement, we can have the feeling that the women of that time were very downtrodden and in many ways they were, but in many ways they were very strong and terribly dominant. You hear in the songs that a lot of husbands live in fear and terror of their spouses. These women went and drank in the pub of an evening and were bawdy, free spirits.

Music hall songs fall into very definite genres. I don't know if it was some strange social quirk of the time, but there are a surprising number of songs, like 'Joshua', that are about girls who made the terrible mistake of taking the young man home and finding that mom has made a great swoop and they lost their young man. There are lots and lots and lots of them:

I used to be as happy as the birdies on the trees
That was when I was courting and my mind was well at ease
I used to be so loving with my Henry at my side
Looking forward to the day when I should be his bride.

Now he's thrown me over and I'm full of misery
Someone else has done me out of William Henry.

He used to come and court his little Mary Ann
I used to think that he was my young man
But mother caught his eye and they got married on the sly
And now I have to call him Father.

There's another one called 'Why Am I Always the Bridesmaid?' sung by this marvellous woman called Lily Morris. Very large, very fat, and it starts with her in a terrible dress and a terrible hat and boots: 'Why am I wearing these beautiful clothes?' She goes on to sing about how she's always the bridesmaid. Twenty-two times she's 'followed the bride up the aisle and twenty-two maidens have answered, "I will", meaning, "I won't", all the while.' When she finally gets a young man, she takes him home and her mother 'Being a widow, she knew what to do.' So she loses her boyfriend to her mother. So you see, toy-boys are not such a new thing.

There is a great deal of another genre—the shabby genteel. They turn up a lot in Dickens—people who are very poor, very threadbare but somehow well mannered—and if you don't look too closely you think they are rather grander and richer than they are. When Stanley Holloway was in NY having a huge success in *My Fair Lady* on Broadway, he went into the studio and recorded a lot of music hall songs, remembering how people had sung them when he was very young. In this song, he sang about being a tramp in Trafalgar Square, which is where four statues of lions surround Nelson's column. He characterized it marvellously; there's rich dignity in the voice. It's a three-act play in three minutes. You only gradually realise he hasn't got two pennies to rub together:

Today I've been busy moving,
I'm all of a fidgety-fidge

My last digs were on the Embankment
The third seat from Waterloo Bridge.

The cooking, and oh, the attendants
Didn't happen to suit me so well
So I ordered my man to pack up, and
And look out for another hotel.

He did, and the new place is 'extra', I vow!
Just wait till I tell you where I'm staying now:

I live in Trafalgar Square,
With four lions to guard me.
Fountains and statues all over the place,
And the 'Metropole' staring me right in the face.
I'll own it's a trifle draughty,
But I look at this way, you see,
If it's good enough for Nelson,
It's quite good enough for me!

The beds ain't so soft as they might be,
Still the temp'rature's never too high!
And it's nice to see swells who are passing
Look on you with envious eyes.
And when you wake in the morning,
To have a good walk for your breakfast
And the same for your dinner and tea.
There's many a swell up in Park Lane tonight
Who'd be glad if he only had my appetite.

I live in Trafalgar Square,
With four lions to guard me.
Fountains and statues all over the place,
And the 'Metropole' staring me right in the face.
I'll own it's a trifle draughty,
But I look at this way, you see,

If it's good enough for Nelson,
It's quite good enough for me!

He plainly had a marvellous voice, but he knew when to sing and when not to sing at all. The verse each time was totally spoken, with quite big inflections. He would go into song and then into speaking in the middle and then he go back into song. That remains a musical theatre dilemma: how do you stop that being a gear change? Yet it's all entirely at the service of the story and the idea strongly gets across.

There's quite a few music hall songs by what in England you might call the 'gormless'—rather vacant, nerdy people:

Since I been courting Matilda Ann
I try to amuse her the best way I can.
Sometimes I take her with me
And count all the gravestones in our cemetery.

Then if we feel like a bit of excitement
Away to the station we wend.
We find a seat on Number 3 platform
And sit there for hours on end.

Watching the trains come in
Watching the trains come in.
We sit and stroke each other's hand
As only lovers understand.

Watching the trains go by
Hearing the porter shout.
When we have watched all the trains come in,
We watch all the trains go out.

There is a very touching, wistful song about a little cockney man who has a small garden in the middle of a built up part of London, but he likes to have the illusion it is a rustic setting. Once when I was working on this song, I had a student who said, 'My great-aunt and great-uncle are the son and daughter of the man who wrote it. Would you like to meet them?' Well, of course I did! And the

great-aunt told me she remembered as a little girl sitting on Marie
Lloyd's knee while her father demonstrated the song. They showed
me a letter from Kipling, who'd written about this particular song,
'This is one of the most wonderful pieces of characterization in verse
that I've ever heard.'

If It Wasn't For the 'Ouses In Between

If you saw my little backyard, 'Wot a pretty spot!' you'd cry—
It's a picture on a sunny summer day.
Wiv the turnip tops and cabbages wot people doesn't buy,
I make it on a Sunday look all gay.
The neighbours fink I grow 'em, and you'd fancy you're in Kent
Or in Epson if you gaze into the mews.
It's a wonder as the landlord doesn't want to raise the rent
Because we've got such nobby distant views.

Oh, it really is a werry pretty garden
And Chingford to the eastward could be seen,
With a ladder and some glasses you could see to 'Ackney
Marshes
If it wasn' for the 'ouses in between.

Remember, there was no performing rights society. They sold
these songs outright for five pounds and that was all the income they
ever got for them. There were two famous songwriters called Weston
and Lee, and every day they'd meet in the pub to write a song.

In the end, radio, movies and television brought about the decline
of variety, and gradually all those beautiful old theatres became
movie theatres or TV studios. And variety died. But then, what's
exciting is that we are now back to square one. We are back to pubs
in London that find they might do better than the pub down the
road if they have a little platform in the corner and have a performer
to entertain.

I'm going to finish by playing you a recording of a song sung by
the genius, Hattie Jacques:

The Bird on Nellie's Hat

Every Saturday, Willie got his pay
Then he went to call on Nell.
Trousers neatly pressed and a new white vest,
Buttonhole bouquet as well.
In Nellie's little hat there was a little bird;
That little bird knew quite a lot—it did, upon my word.
And in its quiet way, it had a lot to say
As the lovers strolled along.
'I'll be your little honey, I can promise that,'
Said Nellie, as she rolled her dreamy eyes.
'It's a shame to take the money!' said the bird on Nellie's hat,
'Last night she said the same to Jimmy Wise!'
Then to Nellie Willie whispered as they fondly kissed,
'I bet that you were never kissed like that!'
'Well, he don't know Nellie like I do!'
Said the saucy little bird on Nellie's hat!